His Rib:

Penmanship Bo
Published by Penmanship Publishing Group
593 Vanderbilt Avenue, #265
Bklyn, NY 11238

Copyright © 2007
Photograph by Karen Gibson Roc
Cover Design by Caitlin Meissner

All rights reserved. This book may not be reproduced in whole or in part except in the case of reviews, without written permission from author.

ISBN- 0-9789695-2-9

First Penmanship trade edition: June 2007

Printed in the United States of America

10 9 8 7 6 5 4 3 2 1

Penmanship Books

Patricia Smith (FOREWORD)	8
Ebele Ajogbe	
Sun/Rise	121
My Name Is Nkiru	123
E. Amato	
Fucking Henry Miller	93
Cristin O'keefe Aptowicz	
Estephania	30
After Reading Old Unrequited Love Poems	32
Radhiyah Ayobami	
Harlem	180
Courtenay Aja Barton	
A Persian Gulf War Love Story	154
First Apartment Poem	155
Felice Belle	
Concrete Thought	191
Un Pequeño Sueño (For Gabriel)	193
Tara Betts	
"The Bitch Poem"	52
Tamara Blue	
I Live Alone	157
Crystal Senter Brown	
16	134
On His Mother's Bed	135
Mahogany L. Browne	
Eliza: The Niece Part II	82

Noose	80
Pied Piper	77
Witching Hour	81

Akua Doku

Le Serpent	177

Eboni

To Begin With	103

Ebonyjanice

Poem For Self-Love	86

Jessica Elizabeth

Fingerprinted	43
Haikus	46
Missing Who?	47

Falu

Mother's Day	50
Helicopters	48

Andrea Gibson

Anything	20
See-Through	25

Nicole Homer

Folded And Shoved	132

Bassey Ikpi

For Peter James Conti	13
"Untitled"	17

Crystal Irby

Revolutionaries Don't Fall From The Sky	171

Penmanship Books

Today I Am Breathing	174
April Jones	
Teacup	110
Amanda Johnston	
History Lesson	107
Over Breakfast	108
Rachel Kann	
Badland Between	11
Erica Kamara	
Bittersweet	163
Rumors of War	165
Abena Koomson	
Time Line	116
LV	
This Sad Love	71
Marie-Elizabeth Mali	
Snapshot	89
Marty McConnell	
Marguerite Porete To Hillary Rodham Clinton	197
Miniature Bridges, Your Mouth	200
Lizzie Borden's Index Finger	203
Derrica Mccullers	
On Loan	63
Gabriela Garcia Medina	
4 Womyn	162
Requiem Para Los Orishas	159

His Rib: Stories, Poems & Essays by Her

Caitlin Meissner
    A Poem For Mahogany   57
    Lasso   61

Aja-Monet
    Ree-Ree   34
    Mother Mae, I Love You Now?   36

Thea Monyee
    Unapologetic   100

Lilian Oben
    The Other Side   54

Lynne Procope
    Flectere: (*Latin: To Bend*)   129
    Rosewater Perfume   124
    The Trome L'oeil Anna Nicole   126

Nicole Sealey
    Mess   88
    Spilt Milk   87

Queen Sheba
    Erotic Haikus   70

Nikki Skies
    Sister SOS   106

Suzi Q. Smith
    Infidelity   195

Sydnee Stewart
    Stranger In A Bamboo House   92

Penmanship Books

Heather Taylor
    How Does It Feel To Be Loved?   95
    Moving Out   99

Kimberly Taylor
    Harlem's Photograph or Why I look At You that Way
    152

Imani Tolliver
    Defending Frida   148
    Miss Carol's House   139
    Ode   145
    Out My Name   142

Kim Trusty
    Burnt Sugar   38
    Babylon Was Me   39
    Black Sweatshirt Blues   41

Genevieve Van Cleve
    Serpents & Stepmothers   136

Jeanann Verlee
    Exhale   112

Megan A. Volpert
    Sad Girls   178

Jaha Zainabu
    Musings   73

Kelly Zen-Yie Tsai
    Poem For Sean Bell   90

His Rib: Stories, Poems & Essays by Her

Women are the mule of the world…

De womenfolks got yo' mule. When Ah come round de lake 'bout noontime mah wife and some others had 'im flat on de ground usin' his sides fuh uh wash board…
Yeah, Matt, dat mule so skinny till de women is usin' his rib bones fuh uh rub-board, and hangin' things out on his hock-bones tuh dry."

>Zora Neale Hurston,
>*Their Eyes Were Watching God*

She pronounced a curse of death on Enki, and Enki's health began to fail. Eight parts of Enki's body - one for each of the eight plants that he ate - became diseased, one of which was his rib.

>*History of Sumerians*

The Genesis creation story is generally interpreted in religious rather than in historical terms, Adam's rib is popularly afforded little more than facetious comments. Ribald males sometimes pun that woman is unfortunately not abreast of man, but only a side issue.

>William E. Phipps
>*Adam's Rib: Bone of Contention*

Penmanship Books

FOREWORD

After a point, it's hard to make one classroom look different from the one before. In the front, the kids lean forward in their seats a little, waiting for you to spit a stanza righteous enough to widen their eyes. Occupying the desks in the center are the maybes—some marginally expectant, others with one eye locked on the sluggish clock. In the back—oh, in the back—are the surly hair-twisters and wannabe thuggies, glaring at you with absolutely no expectation at all.

These kids become your primary focus. It's capturing them that counts.

So that's where she was sitting. Belly shirt strained, dangling earrings of green-tinged gold, heavy greased hair sporting one impossibly red streak. She concentrated on averting her eyes, making sure I knew who I was, and what I had to say, was a little less than nothing to her. She had better things to do—twisting her wild hair to odd peaks, thrusting out her new chest, popping her gum. And although she would die before she would participate in something so dumb, I couldn't stop thinking about her as I led the rest of the class in an exercise designed to help them write out a little bit of their lives.

Once the bell rang, some kids left skid marks getting away from what I'd asked of them; others took their time, stopping to share a story or ask a question. It surprised me to see that my girl brought up the rear, walking as if rushing was *so* beneath her. But I wasn't fooled at all. I'd seen that sullen, deliberate foot-dragging before.

She snickered as she passed me. Just a tiny tooth suck, barely audible. That, of course, was my signal.

"Didn't feel like writing today, huh?"

Her lowered her eyes and muttered low. "Nuthin' to write about." Then she lifted her eyes and rolled them, as if to say, "I can't believe this woman is talkin' to me."

I pondered her throwaway comment, so huge in the room between us. By that time, other students, other challenges, had begun to stream into the room. I had less than one minute to tell her everything. I wanted to grab her shoulders and shake her, to scream into her face, to get her to realize that writing is the only throat many of us have.

Why do women write?

They write because there are doorknobs that twist both ways, because childbirth empties the body, because kisses can be violent. They write because their souls are trapped in shadow, because there's never enough grocery money, because an errant streak sprayed into your hair shouldn't be your only light. We write to counter concrete, because city flowers never grow fast enough.

The talk of the day in that particular school was a shooting that had ended the life of someone most of the kids knew. We write to resurrect the face of a person who is gone, to force breath and voice back into their bodies. We write so that they do not fall so easily into history. And there will be nights when we need to push their memories away from us—we scrawl anguished entries into journals, on the back off cocktail napkins, in dog-eared legal pads, running as fast as we can away from the fact of their deaths. Sometimes the writing does what we need it to do. Sometimes it doesn't.

But even then it's just the act of writing, of dragging that cheap pen across paper or pounding those midnight computer keys, that helps us to breathe and keeps us rooted in the world. When we are writing, it helps to imagine the million of women who are writing too, pasting their lives together with syllable and verb and created rhythm. Think of those sunlit porches, those dark rooms, that stolen moment in the corner of a kitchen or even in the back of a classroom. Think of words languid and desperate, written in graceful script, block letters or mechanical fonts. Imagine that one voice rising, strong like a female country, breathing hard and as one.

Imagine that, baby girl, imagine that.

I don't have time to tell her all that, or even a little bit of it. Instead I gave her one concrete idea, more a writing prompt than a life lesson, and watched as she walked away. She didn't look back over her shoulder at me, as I hoped she would. All that shine, that tarnished gold, that hellified hip swing, the cloud of sugary dime store perfume. I was left slightly deflated in her wake.

Every inch of her was a story. Every inch of her begged to tell that story.

That's the real tragedy confronting us—the existence of a young woman unaware of her sisters and our one throat. What we can do is pray—out loud and on paper—that her winding path leads her into the open circle of our arms.

Or that she someday picks up this book—and hears us call her name.

Patricia Smith, June 2007

badland between

rachel kann

if i knew you from adam,
i could tell myself from eve.
(you can have your precious rib back.)

gladly split atomic,
ricocheted four states away.

here is you:
permitted behind my wheel,
careening back and forth,
one frontier to another.

here is you:
"it is raw power here,
more beautiful there."
"this is erosion."
the whys and wherefores
of intake.

we are twinned watery graves;
try each other on for size.

this is the badland between us.

uninhabitable,
treacherous,
our hearts, always burning like bridges.

here is you:
theorizing on reverse reincarnation.
singing with mccartney.
dreaming of back jumping into a new suit of lennon-skin,
fragile and medicated.

later, your face will screw up into sobs.

i'll press your head against my breast,
envy your safety,
taste my desire to cry.
think of much
i would smuggle across your border.

i've no taste for negotiations.
i gather spilled guts,
tie them into their previous knots.

my heart flops out regardless,
only all distorted,

like

remember me

like

forget i said that

like

forgive me.

His Rib: Stories, Poems & Essays by Her

For Peter James Conti
Bassey Ikpi

i knew it was you who sent the
second line
sent the sudden tender of round
that had me searching for something
softer than cotton
to soothe the fire under my skin
sent the stomach unsettled
the quiet that entered my throat
the rush that said,
"you already know but maybe this will force
your fatigue into rest. your irresponsibility
into organized lines."
still remember the curse you left me with
"we're grown ups now. we change."

i wanted to tell you first
picked up my phone and held it
said your name into the receiver
watched as the phone fluttered and stopped
waited for the familiar click
the woman on the other end
mechanic and hollow
i listen until she reminds me
that you are no longer in service
and i choke a little

because i need you
need to mark my belly
with your hand
to ooh and ahh at the taut
and round it will become
like the day that feels like minutes ago
when you said, 'You'll be the first. i can feel it."
and i laughed at the crazy your tongue creates

remember the way my eyes rolled away from you
"no pete. you will be the first."

and you were. but i forgot
to clarify and i'm sorry
the universe hears what it wants to

And when I changed my mind for the
3rd time
You sent me a Lauryn Hill song
Thrown from a passing car
You already waiting in Zion

reminding me that time waits for no one

And I admit this missing you
Is selfish
but this fear threatens to eat
me from the inside out
when the man i created this poem with
refuses me his hand in comfort
and commitment
you would adopt yourself into this 'we'
and push the lonely from tongue

and i know that you would understand
my vanity
sing for me stretch mark potential
dance my widening hips into the hole
in your side
and praise my growing belly into beautiful
feed me fat and faithful
rock me roller coaster and mood swing
pray me a Lauryn Hill remix
lyrics by Macy Gray
Peter, wish me a girl with your face

a boy with your heart
I welcome your reflection
need to own something that holds your spirit
You wilt me kindness
remind me unconditional
Make me leak with the need to dance
we will always be a rock and rhythm
that no one else can hear
We the stilted memory of
music

you extra terrestrial
you elegba
deliver me a trickster
send me something i can mold into
the you were afraid to become
let me love him like you forgot to love
yourself
like i meant to love you
dizzy and completely
like the lover i could never be
but you held my heart steady as dreaming
my beauty
guide him
hold her
send them on the wave of your memory
reborn
and i will deny you nothing

ask me now if i can hear it
ask me now if i felt you move beside me
ask me now if i can do this for you
ask me now if i can hear you
when this became more than biology
when we became grown ups
i needed you first when the thought hit me
And again when the second line appeared
And again when they smiled a confirmation

Penmanship Books

And again when I wasn't sure
And again when I changed my mind
And again when I changed it back
And again when I realized that she would come
The week after you left
And all I could say was yes
Because Peter asked me to

Laying on our backs in a bedroom that held our quiet
you stretched your arms towards the ceiling
and said, "this is an incantation. you will be the first."
And I said no
When what I meant was
Ask me again when my womb is
Crowded with only this miracle
of missing

when the grief enters
my bones and lives like the converted
i will do this in remembrance
of you

"untitled"
Bassey Ikpi

midnight in the only place
that matters
and i am done fighting

will no longer press you
into scrapbooks
marked
time
will
heal

i promise you

surrender

 and if we're lucky

the smile will be mine
full bodied and promised

own the eyes too
allow me the round
we can share the brown
you can donate the depth
the quiet

 tomorrow the sun shines on
something new
budding in the wake of
necessary
the promise birthed amongst stars

i allow you paralysis

it's sunday
too late for forgiveness

regret

the religion i'm carrying
begs for stronger acts of faith
smooth as the guilt
lobbed at your already battered body

what is your truth?

your legacy beyond the lyrics scribbled onto
the backs of envelopes
receipts
notebooks discarded after the first
honest word

i see you
as i always have

believe you capable
see you shining

even in this
the dark of broken the only
thing that promises safety
need you strength and open
have neither

despite this
i am your protector
breathe life into your excuses
before i give the world permission
to toss you aside

hold on to the hope that
soon you
will smile in this
realize that the universe only gives you
enough to prove your worth

capable

and i have done this before
held goodbyes in the palm of my hand
urging wind the strength to scatter but
not destroy

prevent the running over
this thing frames you
beats in the same staccato
used to push word
and flesh

this is your greatest work of art

don't let it be written without you

Anything
Andrea Gibson

tonight i wanna slit my wrists
hold the blood to god's lips and say taste this
tonight i'd swear even the man in the moon is a rapist
and stars are nothing but scars
bullet wounds from humanity's drive-by
firing at the face of the sky

tonight crying would be too easy
it would please me too much
and no i don't want you to touch me
cause your hands are clean
and i'm filthy

guilty with the blood of something beautiful all over me
i've been weak and leaking so much poison
in all the rivers around me
the fish are dying
and the trees are vying for some light
but i'm the eternal night
writing rhymes about wind chimes and world peace
while even in my sleep
i'm fighting wars that grind the enamel off my teeth
and i wake with my jaw clenched and my body bent

thinking, how many dishes have i broken this week?
in an attempt to not break myself
by taking brutal belt to my hide
cause it's hard to wanna survive
when i know if Gandhi were alive.... he'd shoot me

and all the great therapists of this world might say
maybe your anger is good
maybe your rage is you emerging from the cage
of everything you've been
so i try to be Zen singing mantras of
om mani padme hum
but god fears me too much to hear me
and my heart beats another kid in the candy store
and his mother calls the cops
and every time the clock tics
i start tic tic tic talking more shit
my voice sounding the crucifixion of everything holy
i've got blisters on my tongue
from pounding nails into hearts of prophets
and just when i think i can stop it
Satan resurrects inside me
and everything around me turns to hell
last night i stole pennies from a wishing well
to buy rope
to lynch the last inch of hope from the planet

and all....

because you have a new girlfriend and i can't stand it

and i know it doesn't make sense
i know we decided to be just friends
but i didn't think we'd be just friends forever
i mean...i wanted to be eighty together
wanted to birth poems like babies together
and watch them grow up save the world
cause girl...
you're the only one who could ever raise the sun inside me
and i swear the ground beneath my feet
is only soft because you walk beside
there were times i thought i was so lost
even god would never find me
and then you came up right behind me
and kissed a cross onto my back

and its things like that that got me going crazy
cause i was thinking maybe the breaths we'd take together
would make us live forever
and now you're killing me
look at me i'm dying
not even trying to evolve when
i wanted to be there forty years from now

when the doctor called to say
your mother might not make it another day
and i wasn't gonna be just ok
i was gonna be perfect

was gonna make my love feel
like the first time you rode your bike without training wheels
kneel before you every day
like there was no one else before you
cause i've heard your heart beat like that breeze
that could bring any violence to its knees
and the best lines i've ever written
i plagiarized every word from the thoughts of yours
i heard while you were just sitting in silence

staring up at mars
but you never wish on shooting stars
you wish on the ones
that have the courage to shine where they are
no matter how dark the night
no matter how hard the fight
and how now do i turn away from that light
when i wanted to be eighty with you
birth babies like poems with you
and let them write themselves

was gonna hold your heart to my ear like a sea-shell
til i could hear the tides of every tear you've ever cried
then build islands in the seas of your eyes
so you'd see there's land to swim to
hold your hand and say storms are born
from the same sky we write hymns to when the sun shines
sometimes it takes tempests to wake rainbows
that will wind our pain into halos

was gonna carve your name into my wrist

so my pulse could kiss you
was gonna love you so well

i'd wake every morning
and tell you things like this…

bliss is the moments you're with me
when your gone my life hurts like hell
but i'll do anything to make you happy
even if it means setting you free
to be with someone else

See-Through

Andrea Gibson

we're on our way back to school from gymnastics class
and only in boulder, colorado
my kids are singing john lennon's "imagine"
at the back of the bus
when jesse stops herself mid-verse
stretches her arm across the aisle like a sunbeam
tugs at the hem of my shirt and asks
"what does hatred mean?"

jesse's five years old
anything i say she's going to believe
but i realize i don't know the answer
i'm not sure what hatred means
i could guess and say it's the opposite of love
i could guess and say
jesse, hatred's why there are nothing but white faces
on our private-school bus
but jesse isn't white yet
go ahead and ask her

what color are you jesse?
well… it looks like i'm pink
shane thinks he's orange

skylar says she's tan
rhett says he's see-through...
see, you can see how my veins are blue
but they're red when i bleed...

and i wish there was no such thing as springtime
because i don't trust the machines
that will one day be planting seeds in these gardens
teaching them
some people are flowers
some people are weeds
rip the weeds by their roots
ignore their screams
tilt your own face to the sun
take what you want
you are the chosen ones
        Sitting Bull said white people are liars and thieves
i'd like to tell jesse he was wrong
i'd like to tell her we didn't come like a time bomb
teeth built of bullets
gunpowder on our breath
that this land didn't weep when our feet
first mercilessly hit the ground
i don't want to say we drowned and maimed the children
sliced long strips of their skin for bridal reigns
i don't want to say the moon was slain

His Rib: Stories, Poems & Essays by Her

the constellations dispersed like shrapnel
mother's killed their babies
then killed themselves
when they saw our faces on the horizon
and all that we left was a trail of tears

but if i have to say that i want to say
the boats stopped there
i'd want to say the waves never saw the sails of slave ships
never heard the sound chain links
but jesse think slaughterhouse
think people branded, suffocating, foaming at the mouth
can you imagine what kind of pain you would have to endure
to throw yourself overboard 2000 miles out to sea
Lungs gratefully exchanging breath for saltwater
gratefully trading life for death
       can you imagine being chained to your dead daughter
how many days would it take you to stop
searching her hands for lifelines
to stop searching her fingertips for memories of sunshine
to stop searching her wrists for a pulse
for just some sign of timing turning backwards
to when you just knew
people would never do things like this

and jesse this

is not just a picture our history
not just a picture of our past
we've been hundreds of years
measuring the size of their hearts
by the size of our fists
erecting our bliss
on the broken backs of dark skin
the present is far from gift wrapped
      ask new orleans
ask mothers in the south bronx
chasing rats out of their babies cribs
ask the fathers of the kids
whose lives we exchange for cheap gas
ask our prisons why jail bars always come in black
ask afghanistan palestine iraq
ask the women in thailand who's cancers build our laptops
ask the mexican man working in a field fertilized by nerve gas
ask his daughter when she's born without fingers
or hands to pray with
(ask me how long i could keep going with this list)
god might be watching
but we are not
      you are white jesse
there are bodies dangling
from the limbs of your family tree
our people pull people from their soil like weeds

breathe in our story
force yourself to hold it in your lungs
til you can hear the hymns sung beneath white sheets
til you can feel your own finger on the trigger of the gun
feel yourself fire as they shout
do not look away as bullet enters heartbeat
                    now breathe out
this is where we come from
this is still where we are
now where will we go from here
i don't believe we're hateful
i think mostly we're just asleep
but the math adds up the same
we can't call up the dead and say
sorry, we were looking the other way
there are names and faces behind our apathy
eulogies beneath our choices
there are voices deep as roots
thundering unquestionable truth
through the white noise
that pacifies our ears

don't tell me we don't hear
the moon being slain
the constellations dispersing like shrapnel
don't you think it's time
something changed

Estephania
Cristin O'Keefe Aptowicz

Maybe it was my habitually dirty mouth,
or my habitually dirty hair, or maybe it was
the way cockiness and bragging would prop
their charcoal feet on my irises, mindlessly
stoking the haughty fire of my tongue.

Maybe it was my childhood's lack of ribbons
and Barbies, my zeal at being the only kid
ghoulish enough to slice meaty night crawlers
with my thumbnail for dad's rusty fishing hook,
but whatever it was, I saw myself as boy's girl.

I didn't know what to do with myself when
visiting with female friends: their canopy beds,
their ceramic harlequin masks, their photo albums
made of puffy fabric and glitter paint. Their mothers
sensed my wildness, nervously handling me

tumblers of ice tea destined to be knocked over,
the relentless jitter of limbs, my dirty nails,
the unforgivably sorry mess of me. In the fifth grade,
we met, two pudgy collections of fashion mistakes,
two braying sacks of girl giggles and buck teeth,

and God gave you the impossible task of guiding
me through to womanhood, our friendship tugging me
together when my mouth exploded all over itself,
the gentle counsel of your eyes, the generous salve
of your laugh, the unintentional comedy of our hair.

Our teen years read like a satire on unloveability.
our diaries like racing forms just trying to keep up
with the latest on our galloping resistible hearts.
There were years where we were never kissed,
There were boys who'd threatened the tender

sinews of our shared self, times we wanted
to shattered the mirror of each other's bodies:
I am not you! I could never ever be you!
and yet here we are. Almost twenty years later:
full grown and fleshed out, with love finally

sleeping sweetly in our own beds. On Sunday,
we shared perhaps our millionth meal, banging
our laughs together like ceremonial gongs, and
I marveled at the startling women who sprouted
from such riotous, unstoppable and perfect girls.

After Reading Old Unrequited Love Poems
Cristin O'Keefe Aptowicz

If I didn't think it make me appear crazy still,
I'd apologize to you for having been so crazy then.

Reading the poems I had written about "us"
resurrected all that nervous heat, reminded me

of the insistent stutter of my longing,
how I could never just lay it out there for you.

The answer, clearly, would have been
no, thank you. But perhaps that tough line

would have been enough to salvage
all that was good and woolly about us:

your laugh, the golden ring I'd always
stretch a story for; the pair of mittens

we'd split in the cold so we'd each have
a hand to gesture with; how even now,

the paths we took are filled with starry wonder
and all that bright limitless air. I'm sorry

I could never see myself out
of the twitching fever of my heartache,

that I traded everything we had for
something that never ended up being.

But if I could take anything back, it wouldn't be
the glittering hope I stuck in the amber of your eyes,

or the sweet eager of our conversations.
No, it would be that last stony path

to nothing, when we both gave up without
telling the other. How silence arrived

like a returned valentine on that morning
we finally taught our phones not to ring.

ree-ree

Aja-Monet

she told me
her grandmother
let her
cook crack
on the kitchen stove
   as she squeezed the blunt between midnight lips
exhaling a cloud of hoola-hoops twirling in
the air.

the huge gold-framed hearts

dangling on her ear lobes,

her hair-piece, held

in place

by a blooming red-flowered scarf

the space between us captured our longing
to understand each other
it's amazing how all of our worlds co-exist
with one another
   how separate we'd like to think of them

Biggie played on the radio
and we both nodded our heads
cult-like
to the beat
bobbing our bodies
jerking our joints

"You my bitch, Aja"
crept off the smoke in her throat.
i felt honored.

how spiritual we are--
the way we wound and heal,

in the caves of our hoods
how black and brown girls
gather and peel
comparing stretch marks
and playground scars.
how close we come to each other
never touching
  and when we do touch
--the moment we become physical beings to each other--

it is then that we stand still in our selves
how the soul tap dances and gossips

the secrets
we hide
under our tongues
quiver and creak
like the cockroaches
we chased together

mother mae, i love you now?

Aja-Monet

I am afraid there will come the day
when she will hide pills under her tongue.

23 orange Duane-Reade-labeled-bottles
will tip over the end of the world
at the horizon of the marble kitchen counter-top

two women clothed in black
will lay white lilies
at the skin of the ocean
with rivers for eyes
and deaf ears
for a voice

a brother,
will clench fists and forgive me's
to the heaven
he fears.

And she will swim like the fairytale
she could never be.
And she will dance with God,
tip toeing on His feet.
And she will smile
--dimples--
to the blow of the breeze.

And these two women,
will hold each other
like clumsy sisters,
lovely.

One, will sing
--sultry--

the other,
will pray a poem

--harmonic--

the boy,

behind them,
will try to speak

and she will hush him.

Because for the first time,
she will be pleased.

burnt sugar

Kim Trusty

we ride through rows of cane
as they burn before harvest
our skin turned white from ash
in this St Ann field
I learn that history
smells like burnt sugar

I was twelve
the fire spoke to me
sang a secret, ancestor song
that I wanted to hear more of
so I tightened my reins
walked when I should have run
and scorched my eyebrows and lungs
for a song

I am thirty-two
and no smarter
than that horse loving
fire breathing girl
still getting burnt
by sugar
and a pretty song

babylon was me
Kim Trusty

lover man
I remember
when our minds
shared the same language

tongues twisted and
strawberry sweet
we spoke our history
into existence
saw ourselves
Osiris & Isis
Adonis & Venus
Shiva & Kali
Nimrod & Semiramis

I renamed you Nimrod
son of Kush
son of Ham
fashioned myself
the Babylonian queen
and dreamed
of the day we'd birth
our own Nephilim

but something soured
your strawberry tongue
one day you said
my ziggurats were too high
the next my temples too ornate
the day after that I was exposing
too much of my mystery to the heavens
you said it was Babylon
Babylon was acting uppity
and it was gonna have to go

but Babylon was me

you toppled my tower
with blood and fire
and now all that lies
between us are
funky sheets and
a language so
heavily encrypted
not even our bodies
can break the code

black sweatshirt blues

Kim Trusty

negotiating the social
landmines of home room
I can't school my face
it gives me up soon
as I catch a glimpse of
your lanky black
hooded disdain
you say we can hold hands
at Fairview Mall but
not in the hallways of
Zion Heights Jr. High School
cause everyone's a spy

it's no clearer when we're alone
and our cruel, unrelenting hormones
tangle your fingers in my velcro hair
or catch my bottom lip in your dental work
as we couch wrestle in the basement
amidst the half empty pizza boxes
and your step-dad's Zappa records

you say, this doesn't mean you're my girlfriend

I don't know what it means
exactly all I know
is that when your black
hoodie is balled up underneath
my skinny neck and the smell
of fabric softener and sex is
mixed up in my olfactory there
is nothing you could say
to make me believe
I don't love you

Fingerprinted

Jessica Elizabeth

The words
no longer guttural
more a soft wheeze
escaping the conclaves
of a broken heart.
She says, "If he hits us again he's gone"
and a lawn once lush
held to task by picket fence
begins to brown at the edges.
Wallowing in the back yard
a rusty boiler patched with fairytales cracks open
and shit spews everywhere
The phrase "One more time and you're gone" whirls
Thru the home like a feeble tornado
three children seek shelter
Screen doors slap then stutter unable to close
By age 12 I ascertain
These threats, idle cows
weakened by years of grazing on yellowed grass
no other fields to wander into

And I
do not bother

to lock my bedroom door
My father can pick a lock faster
then it takes a tear to
streak shame across
a bruised cheek.
And I
do not bother
with this mother
stinking of sewage,
her words
shit brown
cannot be trusted.

The boy ripped from me my womb
held it bloody in knotted fist
a scarlet nightingale
a whirring flutter of broken wings.
And I too young to discern that
the pushing and pulling,
The   NO   STOP   NO
would serve only to create
a raw throat come morning.
Futility measured by stains, shit brown
on the stripped bed .
I pried the final "NO"
out of his palm

mewing like a kitten in a burlap sack
as it fills with river water
Realize, it is not even mine
the mattress was filthy when I got here
Empathetic I plunge the sack deep under tide
hasten the drowning.
In the wake of his departure
The words
I   love   you
Churned brackish into dawn
It struck me repulsive
to say the least
And has
whenever I heard
these three words
spoken since.

I often say things I do not mean
or have any intention of following thru with.
I have been known to take things
that do not belong to me.
I am a liar
and a thief

but I am not ignorant as to why.

Haikus

Jessica Elizabeth

1.
Skin of breast unfolds.
Perspiration trickling flood
Your lips wet from drink.

2.
Ice cackles, amused.
Fingertips trace reflections.
Our love mirrored pools.

3. Stole from me my womb
Scarlet nightingale frozen
Blood icicles proof

Missing Who?
Jessica Elizabeth

I have spent the past three years
of my life gathering
scattered kisses like fallen leaves.

      I beg your return.
My soul has grown too heavy
 in your absence,
A burden
meant to be hauled by two.

Ours is a black and blue kinda' love.
              Slow to fade,
A succulent plum
tender to the touch…

Helicopters
Falu

The helicopters are flying low,
looking for the Nikes of missing girls from Bed-Stuy.
Hoping to see their feet in the air, soles to the sky,
lying on their backs for reasons other than death.
Forced to be whore and found, symbol that they are alive.

They are lamp post sisters, whose eyes only meet at night.
Who will tell their mothers their futures look trash bag grim?
Tell their fathers that a man like him, black as ink, sexy like Africa, is torturing his baby into calling him daddy?

I'm scared.
just to place a back pack atop my daughters head,
insurance her mind will remain only on the books.
Take images of bikini clad weeds; show her they were once roses.
Don't tell me her dreams will be discarded like her body,
I can't handle her wearing red heels to school.

Fly the helicopters lower, cause although far in the distance your sons are not exempt.
His eyes follow me in the train station; travel with me everywhere.
Where they dump the bodies.
Where they find the bodies.
Where they use telepathy to locate severed heads.

Torso without spine.

They mutilate your sons,

give two warning shots to the head for your sons.

they son your sons,

make them good Christians,

make him walk with God; son.

Tell your son that he too can be followed home.

Always been a big boy, no wonder he back up the incinerator. That doesn't make him weak,

just proves that rigid bodies do not fold easily.

The cell phone you gave him as protection has been recycled,

why you smell him during your conversation,

He called when he got home, just as you requested.

Land the helicopter if you think outsiders are taking our children.

I doubt. It is we who prey on we. We eat our young.

why do you think the community is silent?

Everyone is too busy chewing.

Mother's Day
Falu

And so, there are no balloons
No celebratory acts for humiliation
No mother's day will come without shame
My daughter asking for her brother.
whose heart still beats loudly in her chest
she has no idea that a baby sits in the chestnut coffin of her eyes
closed casket funeral each time she sleeps,
dreams so responsibly with her brother…

What do I say to my son?
You should have been born in March
with skin kissed into existence and
a collar bone like the father who went head to head with you often,
we spoiled your time here…

And I can't bring myself to lie with legs up,
fearful of inserted fingers ….
Baby, don't think for a second I couldn't feel the hide and seek
Of you
rather drown than hold parents accountable, you
let me sleep at the edge of the bed, my womb will
wait for you to come home, store food for your return, deprive the rest of me as retribution for not
Screaming "yes" at your birth,

and I want there to be more poems like this
would carve you solid frame metaphors
despite being made of disposable incantations.
write finger nails raw, those valuable lines; you
should have released me, excused my behavior a long time ago
damn you for the inability to tip toe around this silence

Brave heart I wish I were stronger,

And didn't speak to your dad with all the passion insecurity has to offer

I bet you believe in monsters,

And will be afraid of doctors and suctions

I threw away my electric tooth brush, surely

you would have been confused the next lifetime

Thank you for sacrifice

Maybe, one day your father will call on you

With more apologizes and

Recognition of your life

I pray he'll learn to treat you into memory,

Let the love poem stuck in his pen be for you

Maybe then, your smile will appear

Shadow your sister at her homecoming football game

Chestnut brown eyes blinking brightly of the introduction to the blood

that is so familiar to yours...

"the bitch poem"
Tara Betts

I am called bitch
because wind wraps around my neck
like lace and I will not be choked.
I drench myself in understanding that mountains
stretch my spine and anger's stench spits out
all the insults insisting I must fall
accept the way men are
not get angry until steam explodes
from my veins
because if I express myself, I will be alone or
the only lovers I might roll in rhythm
with bear hips and wombs,
even though lesbian is not an insult.
I still glide toward the very gender
where some distort my screams,
kick in teeth behind closed doors,
and twist my name into bitch.
      how close can I come to bitch as a name?
      how much are men and women the same?
I claim my throne where men imagine secrets in my tongue
split landscape so I can thrust friction into tunnels
of untainted veins because the dawn's my narcotic
discover new breath in the lungs of sisterhood

spew unwritten letters to my sisters returning to me
because I was taught to believe
bitches don't love each other
bitches back bite, back stab, play the back, get hit from the back
bitches wear little but their skin or be wrapped from head to toe
talkin' about "baby, I love you, you know?"
always proclaiming devotion with uncertainty because
bitches must have confidence sucked from their flesh
their souls savored between arrogant teeth
until bitches begin to relish their title
separating halves of the brain just long enough to let dollar signs and misogyny collapse under gray matter

in defiance, I seek the name unsung
in too many hip-hop songs
I seek the man who loves gumption like water
aspires to be tangled in the lullaby of my womb
sinks into my hypothalamus
makes my neck twitch with memory's touch
he reaches for my grins
when I watch a leaf idle on the wind
his words trace my mouth
he climbs into my aorta
decimates variations of the icon
sculpted into bitch,
then holds onto my heat.

The Other Side

Lilian Oben

If only she could make time stand still and be the partner she knows Lover wants her to be, for just that minute, all would be right in the world. As Lover sleeps, her white dough body rising and falling in its biological rhythm, her own thoughts twist and turn. It will break her, she knows it, but somehow her mind is devoid of better solutions. It's only seven in the morning, but she's ready to go. Lover sleeps, won't rise until ten, if that.

She's quiet so as not to wake her, slips from the bed, looking back only once to make sure she hasn't been heard. Her clothing strewn in all four corners of the room reminds her of her fickle state of mind, as she snatches flung panties, old jeans, faded girl T-shirt, the embossed Welcome to the Moose Motel hidden amid smears of lipstick, kohl liner, other girlie gunk, tugs the clothes on, eyes raking the carpet floor for her phone.

"You leaving already?" A sleepy voice swimming to the surface of wake and she's caught, midway between smashing her left foot into the brown horse hair boot and shoving her phone into the butt pocket of her jeans. She finishes both actions, beat up leather jacket grabbed with right hand, slouch purse flung from shoulder to side with left. A tip-toed walk to the bed, she takes in the naked body, hours old purple marks landscaping her neck and breasts, she's to blame, gets restless again, leans over the otherwise milk-white and hairless flesh.

"Shhh, it's still early, baby," she whispers, best soothing voice on, mind already in the car, gear in drive, speeding 100-fast away from there. "I'll call you later, okay?"

Her lips feel the warmth of sleep as they brush her forehead, praying for no fuss. Not so easy, the eyes flutter open. To quench protest and further delay, she presses a kiss on the ruby mouth, lips plump, breath tart enough to betray deep sleep.

"Get some rest. I'll see you later."

She's striding down the hallway, the moss-green carpet muting her getaway, kicks herself for her weakness. The woman deserves better, she knows it, but she can't seem to let go, wants to keep her around as much as she can, while she can. She burns rubber getting from her side of town to the other. The faster the better, and the other side of town can't get here fast enough. Her hair blows in the wind, the sun beating through the opening in the roof. The promise of the weekend brings a heady buzz as she weaves through the highway traffic, her game's goal never to hit the brakes. A truck cuts her off as she is about to head down the city way and she curses, switches three lanes over without indicating, takes the expressway to freedom. The specter of the city's characteristically low buildings pressed against a clear blue sky never fails to impress her, the governmental blocks and grid map streets leading even the most simple of minds to safety. There's some guilt but she pushes it out, focuses instead on the weekend spreading before her, plans how to use the two days. She knows what Lover had planned, knows what she was cooking up when she invited her over last night, saw clearly, like a face pressed on clear pane, how her mind had thought to trap her for the night, make it spread into Sunday. Soon as she read that sign she made a note to head out at first light the first chance she could. And so she had. The vibration of the phone lying in her crotch makes her jump. Seeing the number on the small screen, she swallows the rise of irritation, debates to pick up or let ring. The better side of her wins and she answers.

"Hey." It's barely been a half hour and already Lover's pursuit begins its suffocation dance.

"Where are you?" The question is the beginning of another one of her girl talks, and she knows it, feels the irritation rising higher already and she hasn't even said much. She makes a turn on to a road she knows well, cuts to the heart of the question.

"I've got stuff to get done, I thought we'd talked about this already." Silence. She knows Lover is on the other end debating whether or not to push the issue, trying to sense what mood she's in today, wondering if this is a good time, and if so, how far to go.

"I can come with you to help, help you get your errands done. We never spend the weekends together. I was hoping we could-" She spies a red white and blue in her rearview mirror and cuts the dead-end conversation short.

"Babe, gotta go. Cops on my tail and I don't have my ear piece. I'll call you later." Then throws a guilty bone, "We'll grab a movie soon, promise."

It's an empty one, she knows and she makes a mental note to talk with her, to tell her. But before she can give the matter any more thought, she's in front of the house, parks the car checking for his on the one-way street, lets herself in with the set of keys. On the entryway carpet, at the foot of the steep stairs, his black size 17 loafers lay strewn, along with everything else that made it off his body or pocket the night before: brushed steel key chain, a birthday gift from her; sterling money clip, crisp bills still clenched in jaws; some loose change.

He's still asleep when she enters the room and she's grateful. The clothes come off, the reverse of their earlier flurry. She throws them on bag in the corner of the room where other clothes, too long kept hostage by the confines of the hard material, stretch out: a creased pant leg, a crumpled skirt hem, the toe of a pointed sequined shoe. In no time, her body curves into his and she is asleep, dreaming of not always having to run out at the first light of day. When he turns over in his sleep, evidence of his own dreams pressed hard into the split of her buttocks, she does not resist. By evening time, she's made the rounds, had time to piece it together, can see clearly how it will go. The small restaurant that she knows is where she heads, moves unnoticed into the corner of the dim room to the edge of the semi circle bar, perches on a bar stool, hooks the heels of her boots on the foot rest. She orders the usual mix and when the ice glass appears, she takes a sip, feels the dark liquid slide down her throat.

Looking around for a light, the pretty bartender smiles, strikes a match to her tobacco rod. She smiles back, remembers how Lover likes to light these for her, sucks in the drug, pushes the smoke out from her nostrils and lets whatever can't make that route take the short cut out the left side of her mouth.

She'll tell her tomorrow.

A Poem for Mahogany

Caitlin Meissner

He asks me,
so, what you doing with your free time these days?
A slick smile gives away everything I have always known:
when there is a hole,
tiny as a pin prick
they'll find it and bear into it
until it gives way to a gaping space
behind the rib cage.

I answer:
I'm writing lesson plans for the masses
and it all started
with my four year old adopted daughter
who was painting the night sky
without stars.

Baby, I said,
go ahead and let the blackness engulf you
fall into the deepest place
for if you just extend your limbs
you may
one day
touch a toe to the very bottom

of the ocean floor.
 I told her,
don't bother being pretty
instead, may you never lose the spirit
that fills your body with endless questions
may the why's blessing your lips
fill the room with your presence
may she never stop dancing
may she always understand
that her motions
are finest
when she is fully clothed and honest.
may she look up to me for the right reasons
and extract only the good.
    I answer:
I'm giving classes to newborn girls
on how to navigate the world--
how to catch
a cat call like a bullet
by just raising a palm
wrap your fingers around it
watch it disintegrate.
I'm teaching the face to make
when bystander's stares
show their fear of your power.
The response, a raised eyebrow asking

what now, mother fucker?

I'm building an army
of a thousand young women
who come with the ego
of a million rap-rhymes
hands cupped over their crotches
head cocked back to one side.
I am teaching syllables:
stand up/
speak out/
move
until fist penetrates brick
heads roll on ground,
eyes dead-wide
lids pinned to the skies.
Cry
'cause there aren't no shame
in a woman's vulnerability
breathe out air thick with solidity
pick up pieces of self
puzzled in a picture that reeks
of your history.
And lastly,
I'm finding the tools,
handing out buckets of concrete

to fill up the holes
pouring bodies that are sturdy
with some wiggle room to grow.
I'm handing out glue to coat skin
so the saying is true,
whatever you say
bounces off/ sticks to you.
I'm building fences around
Brooklyn blocks
creating safe spaces
to play hop scotch in skirts
I've bought all the barbed wire
this borough had to offer
I'm handing out barriers
to keep childhood intact.
Besides that?

I'm trying to quit smoking
pay the rent
stay connected to friends,

you know, the usual.

Lasso

Caitlin Meissner

I'd lasso the stars out the sky
put them in a fish bowl
and present it to you as a gift
if you didn't already own the nighttime.

I know this life only gives us voices
but mine is caught in the cage vocal chords create,
part my lips and out pops
a tiny white flag
waving over molars/
all I can think to say
is that you look beautiful first thing in the morning.

Last year I thought I saw the milky way
in the lines marking the palms of a lover's hands
and foolishly
spoke with loose tongue
because I knew no matter what
I was smarter.

This year finds me full of juice
swollen
unable to lose myself

I can't seem to escape the position
of being constantly available
blame it on technology/

The place where the pillow remains
indented
is a sacred space --
the warm side still smells like you/
the cool side a clean slate.

You caught me just as I was about to learn
the body of a spear shaped shovel.
I'm learning to say no,
because this is important:
I'm burying our insecurities
in pockets of earth.
May the dirt nourish the \
Growth of
Something worth
Talking about.

I'll christen her
Our collective daughter

And she'll have a name as long as the heavens.

On Loan

Derrica McCullers

Sitting at her desk Saloane made a decision.

Late afternoon sunlight swam over the granite façade of the Baltimore Museum of Art and streamed into her office, the warm energy fueling her conviction. There, she decided that she would share her recent past, but only with those closest. She would not cover up the dissolution of her relationship, her self-inflicted isolation or the abortion with lies of bickering, long work hours or "accidents" – respectively of course.

Truthfully, Saloane had no real explanation for her actions during the past two months, just feelings. Clarity was a recently adapted craft, an adaptive process that had not become an available option until the Painting entered her life. It was the painting that brought her to this point and Saloane hoped - now that it would be going to its intended destination - that she would be able to keep the momentum and believe in self-forgiveness.

She wanted to learn what anticipation felt like, instead of the exhaustive fabrications she chose to shape into a "future." Saloane would no longer run from responsibility and commitment by labeling them as monotonous. Life could fall in her lap as it may, she was open. She was growing content with her past and that was more peace than she had felt in a long while. From today on, each time she stepped forward with conviction, compassion and grace, it would be due to the past six days. She would reminisce over this time.

Saloane dragged the tape gun across the box, pressing the tape along its edges, ensuring it was sealed. Closing her eyes, she recalled the details of the painting now locked away in the wooden box at her feet.

Initially, she had welcomed the misdirected package as a distraction from her own thoughts. It gave her frantic mind a place to roam away to. A place other than the space filled with remaining memories of her consolatory two-month pregnancy and teal hospital walls. Ever since the day "The Creation" arrived, a shifting had begun inside of Saloane.

The day it came she was expecting a sketch from a new artist but instead received Aaron Douglas' "The Creation." After numerous phone calls she and her boss discovered that their piece had been misdirected to the Studio Museum in Harlem, a fault of the insurance company responsible for placing the pieces on loan. They arranged to have it picked up on Saturday. For the days in between, it was to become Saloane's sole responsibility and ultimate fixation.

The first day Saloane went home with random details of the picture in her head. Most moments it popped into her mind out of sheer anger. She was furious with the insurance company's incompetence and took insult at the lax manner in which they were handling the situation. It did not matter that her sketch did not need to be installed for another two weeks. It was about responsibility and they had been neglectful.

Most times she would let the anger ride itself out, even after the justifications had lost their weight. The incident had provided a welcome lull in her fits of loneliness and waves of regret. While Saloane's relationship with the piece would evolve over the days to come, that first day she hated it almost as much, if not more, than she hated herself. Especially after all she had done.

Nate had smothered her with affection. Would scratch and grease her hair – almost as good as her grandmother - polish her nails, read her books when her eyes were too tired to focus, and Saloane never really loved him. She knew that now. She stared at a reprint of "Young Man Studying" which Nate had gotten for her last birthday. He chose it because he knew she would like it but also because he found it remarkable how much the picture reminded him of her. Hughes posing, in the "act" of studying, simply to be witnessed in the act. That was Saloane - everyday. Nate knew this about her but never thought it applied to the "us" he loved so much. She had always loved the way he understood her in that naïve way, but

Saloane never loved him.

Often times she felt sorry for him for not knowing any better. Why couldn't Nate see that his energy was wasted on a woman like her? A woman like her could only take and then, could only take so much. Some days Saloane would spend time allowing her mounting frustration with him fester. How dare he place such a burden upon her? How could he expect her to compensate him? Nate gave endlessly, graciously. How could she ever manage to return the gesture? Saloane spent months trying to make it all up to him, she didn't want to be in his debt or ever have him resent her. If she let the love continue Nate would be empty and she would be alone. But reparation was not something she could manage on her own and loneliness was something she was afraid to consider.

In a struggle to protect herself from her fears and baring the guilt of isolating Nate, Saloane lost her bearings and sense of security. To her astonishment the man who loved her was loosening the mooring and was beginning a silent course away from her. While she had been slowly isolating him, Saloane never anticipated that Nate would ever begin a separation of his own.

One night Nate stayed up reading in the widow seat, their favorite cuddling spot in her apartment. Go Tell it on the Mountain cradled in his hands, barefoot, bare-chested, with gray basketball shorts draping his thighs. His eyes were focused on the page, his fingers poised to perform the task of turning pages but obviously not reading. Saloane stood in the hallway shadows, trying to pull thoughts from his head. Saloane didn't remember Nate ever making it to bed that night. The next morning she began not remembering to take her pills. Her and the baby would love him back and share the burden of his love together.

Predictably, Nate was elated at the idea of them having a baby and Saloane went along. She entertained his ramblings and imaginings on what it would be like to be a family. She would even spend time with him making lists of potential baby names. Each time he beamed that smile of his Saloane smiled right back but something broke inside her every time.

There was a yet unshaped life inside her – a mass of multiplying cells and DNA transmitting signals within her womb – but she didn't feel like it was, or would become, anything that belonged to her. It was for him and, while it was still early, Saloane was not certain even this was something she could give Nate. There were moments, quiet, optimistic and fleeting when she thought about really wanting to be a mother. She practiced expressions that she remembered seeing on her own mother's face. Expressions she hoped would get easier and come naturally. But nothing felt natural. Perhaps, with enough practice and preparation Saloane could have convinced herself into the part of a lifetime but Nate interrupted her progress with the idea to use material from the window seat cushion in a quilt Saloane's mom was making for the baby.

 The window seat was for the two of them, not the future family of three Nate gushed about. It became apparent to Saloane that the baby would not help relieve her of the stress of loving a man; it would simply ask more of her. It would be one more person whose loving gazes and outreaching arms she would not be able to fill. Saloane, without consulting Nate or her mother, made an appointment with her doctor and had an abortion. She knew it would mean the end of her relationship but she all she could think of was rest.

Her head lay on the desk as she fought back tears. More than anything, the gaze and the touch of Dr. Brooks had been the hardest part of the experience. Until that moment Saloane had been convinced that she was completely detached.

Dr. Brooks sat staring at Saloane in her paper gown. She offered out her hand. After long seconds of it floating there, empty, she firmly took Saloane's hand into her own. "Have you really thought about this?" "Have you talked to anyone else?" "Have you even spoken with the father?" Saloane hated the questions and turned cold. "This is about me and I need for it to happen this way," she said, "I've decided." Dr. Brooks' face sloped into resignation as her hand slid away from Saloane's. "The nurse will be in soon."

A shallow pool of tears had formed on Saloane's desktop. She dipped her finger and swirled them around on the mahogany. Saloane cried because she knew she had been misunderstood and it was too late. It was true that she was not ready for the baby, and would have become a mother for all the wrong reasons. But where Dr. Brooks' glance had gone wrong was in the assumption of callousness. Saloane wished the hand that was offered to her that day held the strength to allow her to face the responsibility of her choice. Instead she only saw it filled with pity, accusations of immaturity and the heavy finality of loneliness if she did not change her mind. That was something she could not accept. She simply wanted the open space to think it all out but quilts, baby names and early twilight gazes across pillows with her lover did not allow enough space for thought, or understanding.

The painting had been different.

On her second day with the painting Saloane dedicated the majority of her time to zealously committing its colors, patterns and aberrations to memory. She felt welcome in the vastness of its borders. The forms and hues made themselves readily available but gave her space to still view herself. The first few nights the work accompanied her home on the bus. Making her way down Charles Street, Saloane would recreate its forms on the fabric of her skirts with her fingers. The fields of grass sloped over her thighs, a brown hand stationed in heaven at her knees, and a man stood at the center of sky and earth. People looked at her funny, many probably assumed she was a client of one of the many mental health offices occupying Charles Street. Saloane never let it bother her. She welcomed the associations with instability.

Late moments the two nights following the arrival of the painting, Saloane would stand at her canvas imitating the movement of Douglas' work - the slight flicks of his wrist, and what she imagined to be the hunch in his back when he painted the arches and spheres of color in his "Creation." She admired the apparent ease of his steady hand. In those moments when Saloane would struggle with memories of the abortion, she would replace Dr. Brooks' hands with those of Douglas. The doctor's eyes no longer bore reluctance. Instead they were confident, consoling. These new eyes understood the path of things, understood that this was all part of a larger plan. A mere aberration in a more beautiful work. On the third night, Saloane added specks of red at the feet of the brown figure and fell in love with the work and the baby she had sent away.

On the fourth day with the painting, Saloane worked steadily through the work hours. She placed calls to everyone on her notepad, ate a healthy lunch. She even called her mother and genuinely enjoyed her anecdotes about the ladies of the deaconess board at her church. While Saloane had always envied her mother's ability to be completely candid, she thanked genetics for not endowing her with Ellen's naiveté. If anything Saloane was stubbornly realistic, callously practical. But recently, Saloane found herself lost in the possibility of things, most often during the quiet moments she spent with the painting.

At this point she could paint its sky with any medium - charcoal, pencil, watercolor. All of it felt and looked natural to her. She found herself most captivated with the stance of the brown figure and the undulations of his earth. Saloane reflected on the movement of light reflective and its source, which she had yet to determine. She could not determine if it emanated from the soft hand in the heavens or from the lone individual occupying the field.

Saloane's days had flown by, work seemed effortless and her time spent at home became less frustrating. The entire act, she realized, was an experiment in a parallel life. She had never been particularly nurturing, hadn't even been capable of pinning the diapers of baby dolls, most times only drawing her own blood. She remembered one day packing up her dolls and spending her "play time" on her mother's bed reading.

Saloane sat studying the Black-Eyed Susans on the museum lawn. Her sparsely decorated office gave her a perfect view of the spring blooming in the city. She sat waiting for the courier to buzz her line, letting her know a messenger was there to pick up the package. A painting that was not intended for her but was now a part of her. It was weaved into the pale greens of her head scarves. Had planted its browns in the lines of her fingers. Cloaked her in its mute yellows, pinks and blues each time she dressed for work.

That morning, for the first time since her mother took out her braids with their rainbow of beads at the ends and let her go natural, Saloane felt satisfied with herself. She was finally peeling away the remaining layers of discontent and incompleteness. For so long she had been dissatisfied with the people in her life, but the recent days spent inside her revealed to Saloane that the only partial work had been herself. Now she could finally see where to begin the process of filling in the lines. The endeavor would be restless, but as she sat at her desk, with the boxed Aaron Douglass painting at her feet, Saloane felt assured that she would withstand.

One brown figure stood on earth. In his "Creation" he stood alone without loneliness. Much purpose lay in his solitude. The layered rings of color, the hand of God rippling with the strength of human possibility and signs of life to come. In his solitude she felt comforted, felt the rush of warm milk with cinnamon from her mother's stove and the call of " 'Loane" from her sister on younger summer days. That morning, her last private morning with the piece, she stole. She stole strokes of the brown from the figure's broad shoulders and proud neck. She took his radiantly muted surroundings, took it all and cloaked them in femininity. What at first fit like a hand-me-down handed down to soon, on this morning was second skin.

The silver clock on Saloane's desk read 3:37. The package was expected in the shipping and receiving dock by 4pm. She looped string around the box one final time, tugging, ensuring its sturdiness. Crossing out the day on her agenda, Saloane prepared to leave. Reaching for the portrait and then the light switch, she smiled at the thought of the early mornings spent with the piece. Closing the door she felt a burst of what felt like anticipation, there was so much to come. Saloane stood a bit firmer than she had six days ago. Her shoulders set wide, body healing and eyes ever aware of the future, she could feel the relief of forgiveness and faith rush over her. Passing a smile down at the "The Creation" in her hands, Saloane switched off her office light, finally ready to set out.

Erotic Haiku's

Queen Sheba

1.

Good dick is hard to
Find if you keep looking with
Your eyes not your hands

2.

I still think of you
Laying still hot sweaty in
afterglow (of) new men

3.

Come dream with me on
Clouds that float over waters
Landing on our lips

This Sad Love
LV

This sad love that breaks my heart
breathes softly in my ear.
Copper curling beard gentle rough on my nape.
Held all night long, slowly I wake to
mingled scents of sweat, sex, faded cologne.
Soon I will slip out, undetected at this hour,
returning with coffee you are too sleepy to drink.
Only partly aware you will find me,
snuggling in, sighing, almost smiling,
as I try to take one more sip.
My eyes half shut against the morning, dreamy,
because you break my heart.

This ache spreads out from chest,
a heart split, pumping itself down limbs to you.
Fear of loss burning back to center.
I am too old for youthful dreams.
Not deluded by these blissful minutes,
I know we feel love more fully
when we understand bereavement.
You are not here every day
yet while you sleep, peaceful,
I imagine that you might be.

That my eyes would open each morning
to a security gone more than once.
I try to let it go, live for today,
but I yearn for control,
for the certainty of plans and promises;
and against my will I test you.
Dragging you out of sleep,
fingers caressing your beard, I whisper,
Will you stay if can't date on school nights?
Will you leave if I have to work weekends?
Should I walk away before you feel trapped?
Should you, before your lust fades?
Do you realize how frightening it is that I love you?
For you, not just for me.
You are too tired to play my game.
Troubled, yet you kiss my lips
and believe in the simplicity of the present.
Too comfortable to want my coffee,
You have the healing power of holding.
I search your face
but see only drowsy confusion
caused by my insecure ramblings,
and I know this moment is perfect.
All the future is a mystery.
So I turn my head and press my cheek
against happiness that breaks my heart.

musings

jaha zainabu

today i heard a gunshot in the
alley under my window
i am not wise to the makes and sizes of guns
i am a poet   an artist   a mother
three shots to be precise
not just me
somebody else hadta heard it too
it is three in the afternoon
a sunny day
june
these are the things that
riot my headspace when
i endeavor to write about
grandmothers   garvey   drums

my poems are little now
perhaps someone's life has ended
but no one has missed a beat

at the liquor store
crazy melvin is begging for change
rolanda the crack head is selling pussy
in unit b demarco is smoking weed

the couple downstairs is making love
and i am listening because it is beautiful
i imagine she lays face downward and grips
the headboard tightfisted
while he is stroking inside of her
long   thick
the cushion of her backside is
christmas   merlot   rent paid
the fucking is good
i am never short of stories on buckingham rd
an elegant name for a street with such drama
even more ironic that it intersects king

yesterday someone pissed in the hallway
the ice cream truck comes by after dark
and last october the brothas set off fireworks for two and a half hours
starting at one in the a.m.
i would like to blame this on the white man
it is eleven p.m. and i am up writing
because that is what i do
but i am in search of the who of who i am
on this saturday night in los angeles
where someone is being asked to dance
bishop collins is preparing his message
and good times don't come on local networks no more
maybe michael was too black too strong for tv

thelma too gorgeous to be nappy and brown skinned
and i surmise they killed off james
because white america couldn't handle
a black man sticking with his family
through bad times

i am writing

and the musings and prophecies just come
like wednesday before last
the children were out front playing
two boys and a girl on one side
three boys to the other
a volleyball type game
except there was one child in the middle
in my day
    i am old enough to have a day
we called it keep away
now   monkey in the middle
this is believe i can blame on the white man

but life in the hood ain't always bad
like on fridays hank the dealer buys
books and balloons and toys and food
for the children who don't have very much
and the grandmamas and granddaddies are

addressed as ma'am and sir
the peace and sage sistas are queens and miss ladies
and lil' andre carries the groceries for
mama jerome when her boy ain't around

but the splendor of moments like these
and more are shadowed by my neighbor
claire
getting the fuck beat out of her by her boyfriend
i don't know his name
every kick follows a stupid bitch this
every slap a silly muthafucka that
and i am so sorry that i cannot make her have a better life

still my mind wanders
and i fanc-y leimert park recalled little africa
where all of the businesses are black owned
    for real this time
the young sistas in training eagerly receive
council from the she elders on
hoochie coochie fryin' chicken and being grown
while the he soldiers are braided dashiki'd
and employed
 it is saturday night in the jungle and i am just
writing

Pied Piper

Mahogany L. Browne

If you are reading this

It is too late
Your bones hurt with the irony of knowing
He is not coming home
Not coming to bed
Not sleeping in your embrace,
Again.

Face the music when the sun rises
Falter your footsteps to the kitchen, the bathroom – the front door
Look back and compromise – once more
Say this is the last time

The last time you'll love someone so much you forget that you ever wanted something tangible:
a note, a hug, a kiss, a tug at your braids, a pull for your hips
something that says you aren't crazy for feeling the dementia,
that shreds your nervous system into confetti

Dye your insides fuchsia and forget the blues ever existed
You never liked them anyway
Not even when you showered together
Or when you read the paper – line by line as if his words and your

tongue were born like this
And now you know, the silence
the prelude of all that jazz
the swing and swallow of dead men walking/writers

You fell in love with a poet
and blame your mother for not telling you
There will always be another stage brighter
than the one in your bedroom
Than the one that connected your eyes to each other
Across the room…that night

You will always believe in him
More than the words he's stitched to papers himself
SOS'd his soul in between the lines
     But, this is not your cue

     You will never save him
The phone calls from across the country are
lifelines sucking away your verve's core
He loves you enough to not kill you
But, mentally…
   He's already sharpened the sword.
   Samurai swung at your skull
   And watched your eyes spiral in the wind
I wish this were a metaphor

It's nothing but plain old English truth;
He was never your God,
Who promised to save your soul, after the altering of your altar

I wish this were a metaphor
It is nothing but plain paper bag and shoeless truth;
He is of no cloth that will bring pride to African Kings

He is too beautiful and brilliant and cunning for you to notice
    The malicious tongue
That darts between his lips while singing you the same song
He sang for her in Japan, London, Los Angeles, Texas and New York

The words may change,
But the melody is as clear as the flutist stealing
Children from their home:
Empty beds taunting the graves with bare coffins

Lucky you...
        To sacrifice the movement of free will
and shuffle your feet from an awakening so pure
Tell me how much it hurts to hear these words
Find a mirror
Trail the reflection of a woman who
looked like you, once.
Except, she was something special.

Noose
Mahogany L. Browne

She spilled tears across my face
praised the heavens like
they could save her from my vengeful grip
I never start the madness
instead they employ my unbiased hands to do their dirty work

All she did was dance in the night
turned apples to cider
when moonlight slumber couldn't keep her
… I watched
sure they would trail her footsteps of freedom to a halt

… Sometimes

I moved with her
let the wind carry my torso like paper
like feathers
like lover's hearts a flutter

I moved for her
until I heard their footsteps
watched them snatch away her smile
stifle her spirit
bound by fear until she dangled in my reach
whispering

How even my grip couldn't block her view of the moon

witching hour

Mahogany L. Browne

when the clock strokes midnight
i will whisper you a reason
keep my bosoms to the moonlit wind
and wax your feverish breathing

most men run from thunder, so dark
it slits a permanent crease into the
shadows
so we forgive the masculine soul for
fearing the unknown

and still you wonder of what lies beneath
these dressings
where i lost a grip on his fingers
misplaced his first digit and thumb
like a roll of quarters

close your mouth, help
me find them

before the sun follows our movement
from slumber
copy my fingerprints, you carbon man
awake with fire on tongue

curse me holy
before tossing my teachings to the dust
this womb
was built
to understand

Eliza: The Niece (Part II)

Mahogany L. Browne

She never treat me no different than the rest
My wavy long hair ain't mess her over none
She love me like she made me
More than my momma could, I reckon
Her smile never parts ways when she see me coming
Like the rest of 'em
Say I'm half devil girl
Say I think I'm high and mighty
Forget we used to play mud pies together
And under all that brown sludge – no one could tell us apart

Antie love me though
Like I ain't never felt
Tol' me not to wait for no man
Go out and make a way for myself
Make a way for our family
Tol me to never mind they bickering
Just keep the lord in my heart
And the prize...
    She tol me the prize was whatever I wanted it to be
Used to sing to me while combing my hair
Patting pads of oil into the thick bushy curls
Sangin' songs just fa me

When I gets old enough to work in the bar
She come to see me
I loves it there
All that sanging and cussing!
Even when men folks try to feel on me
Try to touch my parts like they owned me
I figure it's worth the songs you hear...
   ...the laughter you feel...
Sides, if I's nice enough, they leave me be
'Cept one of 'em, dey calls him Sin...
Cause he always up to no good
Sin wouldn't stop messing with me
Wanted to smell my britches, that's what the other girl's said
Hell, that's what his eyes said ... all cock eye'd
Them girls tol' me he was a good catch – for any colored girl
But I ain't want no parts of him – the way he look at me like
Half-priced meat on Sunday
'sides my Antie say fast girls finish last
I never got what she was saying until I watched one of them girls
Making time with a mister in the alley
she don't get tips no more... got to wait nine months or so before
she come back – but then the other girls say ain't nobody worth anything
goin' want her den'

but them songs – them songs they sing in there remind me of my Antie, her voice like god's gift to me

I talked her into coming to see me one night
She came in her big dress
with her big hips switching like those thick branches
by the outhouse
Antie got a way of stopping people's from talking
even when she just in her rags
that day – she came in them doors right when the other singer
turned up sick backstage
and I begged Antie
please, let 'em hear you sang
sing anything!
She just shushed me and sat down staring
At all the people
That night Sin was in a forceful mood
Told me he was goin' make me his, one way
Or another
My Antie heard that and her eyes caught a flame
Turned a color I ain't never seen before
She walked up to Sin and pulled out her blade
Said, you unhand my niece
For I make you another neck, sir
Sin got quiet
So quiet I could hear his blood moving
And everythang went still
Even the music ain't played none, least not to me
And my mind went blank

And Sin kept still

And Antie looking real calm said, thank you sir

Sin walked out them doors so quick – I thought he would

Fall from the wind blowing behind him!

Antie sat down, stirred her tonic with her index finger

Took a swig

Then said, hell – I'mma sing tonight

I'mma sing like you want me to baby

(excerpt from Eliza: An Ekphrastic Series)

Poem for Self-Love

ebonyjanice

I am smiling
because my ancestors
might be proud of this poem
this prayer for the intangible
this piece to bless God for the unimaginable
even throughout all of my sin
I am alive
I am grass stains on white Capri's
still marching in the "Thank You I Know I Look Good" parade
I am not yet "in love"
though I have experienced something close to it
So heavy on my chest his presence rested
that I decided to let him stay there
in the memory of my heart
but "he"... he had to go
he wanted to just play video games, have sex and dream of football
while I wanted to boycott BET, write books and make history
I wanted to tell Jamie she is lovely
let Alystia know she should still love
tell Kelly to move on cause life goes on and Jason would want her to live again
so This piece is for colored girls,
negro women,
black chicks,
African American princesses,
dark skinned white fillies and sassy Latinas
You who always were
and you who always will
This is for you to simply remind of self love...

Amen

Spilt Milk
Nicole Sealey

uncle tongued his first niece.
father bit his only child,
their tongues tickled loose teeth or
empty spaces where they will grow.
do you know how to kiss? They asked.
"uh uh," sighed the *everygirl.*
want to learn?
everygirl has a story:
obscure wanton kisses,
pieces of her misplaced in mouths
of uncles and fathers.
only eight,
(and some say, "in a moving dream")
she'd come downstairs for a glass of milk,
unwelcomed petting.
fancies of
first kisses no longer pretty,
lips hardly delicate.
her secrets had been told:
everyman's mouth of a relatively related taste, while
half-empty glasses of milk lost flavor.

mess

Nicole Sealey

blood pursues threadbare Cherokee jeans
wetted fabric patterning red mess—halls
books like foundation mask blemishes her age brings

they fall down, Breath, Eyes, Memory falls down
not before imprint of genes marked them grown
communion: crimson ballpoint pens, white napkins

skateboard stunts and sudden stomachaches
ink blots—stretched blood clots
stain, thick mass formless shape
cardinal ponds brand tomboys' denim memory

motionless, chaos streams down thighs
strippers' meticulously slow slide down poles
soiled legs that when sleep cramp, cramp,
cramps now.

Snapshot

Marie-Elizabeth Mali

My husband emails me a close-up photo
taken with his cell phone on the airplane
about to take off in an icy rain.
The look on his face is tender. Consistent
as he is in his expression of love for me,
I more likely follow a day of closeness
with a well-timed snap.
Everything changes, everything dies:
May this truth be a doorway, not the armor.
Marriage, too, is a kind of dying.
The more I die to who I think I am,
the more myself I become.
I look into love's benign, shattering face,
those eyes I want to remember, to mirror,
and save the photo in case the plane goes down.

Penmanship Books

Poem for Sean Bell
Kelly Zen-Yie Tsai

my imagination finds you
i dream you speak to me

    tie me up -- you say --
    each part of me
    in good-smelling bags

    like the kind my girl's girl gave away
    on her wedding day

    i think it was
    lavender
    she said

    please
    don't tell my babies how i died

    i didn't mean
    to make her a widow

    wanted better things for us

    to make it up to her

    don't know
    how many bullets
    hit my body

    except that
    it was enough

    all i could taste
    was the flavor of
    cherry pop rocks

on my tongue

all i could smell
was snatches of
hot skin and rain

don't know where they're
taking me now

just paperwork after
paperwork

these bureaucratic fools
are up here too

they keep asking me questions

as if i'm gonna remember something

but i'm glad that i don't remember

because memory would be too much

stranger in a bamboo house

Sydnee Stewart

you look familiar through rose colored glasses
I think I remember you from childhood
Red oriental dolls dance to rituals and bad habits
burn like cigarette smoke scented with jasmine incense

There's a stranger awake in a bamboo house and
it's quiet like Christmas, a birthday or any other holiday where
conversations are kept cordial
There is silence that only felines hear
the kind that roam alone in jungles made of concrete
This stranger sleeps alone wishing for wings
This stranger can't run outside, the doors are locked from the inside
This stranger sings songs she learned in the asylum
where food was served on bamboo trays
This stranger is afraid for her unborn song
The kind felines hear when motherhood or breast milk are near
This stranger eats with chopsticks made from glass
This stranger sits at the altar on knees bent looking
there is no resemblance in the reflection
the spirit of this stranger is made from cheese cloth and

the seam of its soul wears no designer label
This stranger arrives bearing flowers and burdens
from wisdom the presence of
This stranger is uncomfortable in this place that

used to be called home

It seems the heart of this stranger

has been evicted, convicted and redeemed.

Fucking Henry Miller
E. Amato

Read Miller for two hours. Page 160 to 210.
Slow read, like human speech.
I could read all day. It is a frenzy.
I roll around the bed with him in my left hand
and slip my right hand in my panties.
I want to fuck him
so I tuck my right hand in my panties,
imagining the Real of him.

      The story envelops me,
      I am one of his Cunts,
      but a good one, a smart one.
He tells me his story
and then I am Her, the one he is fucking.
I am her, I am her, I am her
until it all explodes & I have fucked him
in the vestibule /on the carpet /on my back
::Rita ::
I have stolen her name her Time her hair
he has reached across pages to me
across Death // there is no death
there are only Words.
Words animate

Penmanship Books

dance me into
a life that is his
I have stolen the space she inhabits
right there, on the carpet, in the vestibule
I am She –
the Cunt of his dreams
like he is he wrote across 80 years to fuck me

All his words are where they will lay
so he can lay me down across decades
he satisfies me

his words all written but
my keystroke explosions still to come
changed after fluids exchanged
disguised as a redhead spreading her legs
holding him in my left hand
as my breath quickens
as my body opens
as my words cease
as I sit in his lap on the rug in the vestibule

exhausted

Reality is just a starting point
Flesh is fabricated from words.

HOW DOES IT FEEL TO BE LOVED?

Heather Taylor

Ellie

The calendar is tacked up beside the fridge. Your mom makes sure to send it every year marking carefully the birthdays of relatives dead or still living. Remembrance, she says, is all we have. You keep a small white candle in the drawer reserved for take-away menus, batteries and broken pencils. In your room by the window, you settle on your knees – the floor a checked reflection of hospital corridors. The cold seeps up your nightgown, settles in your lungs, your chest heaving. You lean forward, knees pressed into the floor, the candle placed and lit. The light flickers, reaches out in the glowing darkness and bathes your face. You glow like the Madonnas at Sunday mass.

The click of beads subdue the swoosh and whirl in your head as you mumble under your breath. Your hands are clasped like he held yours that day, clammy and tight until all you wanted to do was pry them apart. Wipe away his panic. But you were too afraid to let go so you held tighter. Seven years on and all that's left is dots on dates that matter to no one. A birthday that only exists in your alternate back to the future. Another reason for a little dress hidden under beds in boxes. Your remembrance.

Emily

You get invited to a party. A proper party with boys and food and videos. You still have the innocence that comes with that pre-teen age of 13...drinking won't come into play for you for another couple of years yet... Your mom seems to know how to play it right. Maybe a trick she learned growing up? In any case, she knows she can't drive you to that party. That it was one of those times that even getting out of bed was painful. So she orders you a taxi. A taxi! A taxi! You've never been in one before. Growing up in a small town, people you knew didn't take taxis. Taxis were only taken in movies by posh people or powerful New York lawyers. They weren't for girls going to their first party ever. That was luxury. But it was ordered and on it's way.

You stand at the front window trying not to jump up and down as each car passes, trying to keep your eyes trained casually at the road and not craning your neck to try to look around the corner. And then there it is. A yellow taxi. "Mom. I'm going. The Taxi's here" Everything is blurry, like a dream. Did she hug you? There is money in your hand and you are out the door and by the curb. The driver lifts the handle and you are suddenly a princess.

It's strange to sit in the back, the material a dark smooth velvet. You breathe out the address, your normal boom reduced to a mutter and as you drive, you keep your hands tight together to keep yourself in. You read every sign and bit of writing in that cab. Just try to soak it all up. Not until years later will you realize your mom didn't know how important that day was. How special you felt for that 15 minute ride. Like the world was at your feet. That finally your Mom thought you were really grown up. That not once during that ride did you think it was only because she couldn't drive you herself.

Rebecca

846 metres. That's what the sign says as you board the elevator. Your stomach jumps as you express your way to the top of the CN Tower – the tallest in the world. You still have nightmares about buildings this high, worry about kamikaze pilots, wonder if Canada's foreign policy is safe enough to let you go to the very top. There is a decisive ding and the doors open. Your high heel tilts dangerously close to the floor and you brace yourself – palm flat to the edge of the metal doors.

"Are you alright?" Red faced, you mutter yes to the deep voice behind you and inspect the floor as you move into the crowd of tourist bulb flashes. You circle the deck once, twice, three times. The multi-lingual signs have been read in triplicate as you watch children tiptoe their way onto the transparent viewing floor afraid they'll fall through, their screams dissolving to laughter when they can dance their way across the sky.

You stand at the edge. You know it's safe – your brain understands there's no way the thick glass will turn to nothing so you'll fall through space and take out a tour group on the sidewalk below. Not one of them noticing your near dead body hurtling downward through space like a bottle rocket until it's too late.

It won't happen but still you stay at the edge. "Let me help you." The same warm voice from the elevator breathes itself into your ear and you feel a hand cup your elbow. Your eyes move from the sheer drop ahead to his face. He is smiling. Your mouth mirrors his and your teeth feel air for the first time in months.

Without a word, he leads you into a shuffle side-step and suddenly you are there - on the glass divide. Like the children before, your laughter rings out breaking the boundaries you thought would never be crossed again. His e-mail address destined to be buried in your pocket, yours in his.

Tom

Her nametag says Sally printed in hasty male writing - the only remnants of a year ago manager whose friendly handshakes turned to caresses to an overnight dismissal. Her shoulders slump under the uniform made for a bigger frame, faded by too many washes and a limited budget. Your trolley squeaks alongside the conveyer belt, its left wheel a lazy eye wandering to the right. A constant bang into the side of the aisle. The grey-hair in front recounts the change painstakingly put on the counter and Sally stares at the ceiling - she's seen this episode too many times. You realize you are holding your breath as you watch the interchange, your hands white knuckles on the trolley handles.

The scanner beeps two men's shirts, one pack of boxer briefs before her fingers roll the cotton of a baby snuggle, aged 3-6 months. A second passes and she looks at you for the first time like you're a lost friend instead of a missing lover. A father newly born in the check out line.

Chloe

It's either loud or quiet. You feel sad today so your orgasm ripples out in tiny waves from your centre leaving you quiet. Speechless. He thinks he's done it wrong. "We'll try again" But it's happened. It's deeply personal. You can't tall him it's like a salvation. That his soft touch brought you a relief you didn't know you needed until you were there. In his bed. The light held back by heavy curtains. Your bodies moving over the landscape of pillows and duvets, blanketed by shadows.

You lie there, your moment come and gone. It's different every time. You try to explain the feeling. Your fingerprints trace circles on his back like they did in childhood when you played with spilled sugar on a Formica table top – the remnants of sugar water coffee experiments as your parents tried to keep their vocal cords stretched to normal tones. Red faces that would stay permanently so until the spectre masquerading as fatherhood slammed the door goodbye a few days later.

In the tangled sheets, his sigh shudders through you spooned, sweaty drifting. Words finding empty pockets in meaning like the plans in your head.

Anchorless and looking for home.

MOVING DAY

Heather Taylor

I took shared bills and my engagement ring
as a promise we'd live here
until one of us died;
grey hairs left on pillows as after thoughts

Instead I thumb through the remains
of martially shared CDs, gaps
like broken teeth in racks on the wall
we hung in a shared DIY frenzy.

Like an overzealous librarian,
my friend reminds me about the Clint Black
and James Brown she lent me:
There's no way he's havin' them.

Penmanship Books

Unapologetic

Thea Monyee

I was not a damsel in distress when he met me. I was living in a castle I rented, driving a carriage I paid the note for every month, and perfectly content spending an evening alone with a lit candle and Tracy Chapman's scriptures playing in the background. I always kept my windows open. I always took long hot baths, and I always knew I would not become the type of woman who relied on a man for her happiness.

When we met I was beginning a small tour for Def Poetry to promote the show's first season. I was dating four men, very casually, and I called all four after my first date with him and explained to them that their services were no longer needed. I knew I had found THE ONE.

As we approached our wedding date I can remember people asking me if I was nervous. My father even told me it was not too late to change my mind as we were walking down the aisle towards my future husband. I knew it was nothing personal towards him; it was just that my parents' marriage did not end on the best of terms. But there was not a shadow of a doubt in my mind. I told my father about the time my husband left for Ethiopia for two of the longest weeks in our relationship. When he returned home he told me the one thing preventing him from continuing a relationship with me is that I was too quick to give up my power. He said that I needed to participate in the relationship and understand that his needs were not the only needs that mattered. I remember this only made me adore him more.

At the time I thought he was merely mistaking my kindness for weakness. Over the course of the next three years, and two beautiful daughters later, I am just now beginning to scratch the surface of the part of me he recognized then. The part of me I refused to own, yet somehow it managed to taint everything that I thought I was as recent as two weeks ago.

Some women begin to shrink at the beginning of the

relationship, others shrink at the altar. I believe I was gradually shrinking the whole time, but it accelerated with the birth of our children. I wish I could tell you the exact moment I started feeling the pressure, but the truth is it does not hit you over the head like an ACME crate in the cartoons. It is more like a fog that rolls in quietly, and before long you cannot see your own reflection when it is right in front of you. Before long you are acting out of a fear of being exposed to an imaginary, yet very powerful, group of judges who are waiting for you to prove that you are an unfit wife and mother. The expectations you have for yourself begin to distort and everything begins to feel like a test of your womanhood. Don't ask for help, they will think you are weak. Don't complain, they will say you cannot handle it. Don't leave a shred of evidence that you are not enjoying serving the needs of everyone around you. Don't ask for anything because you will look selfish. You should be able to handle this, and if you can't, then you are a failure.

Recently I began to experience the burnout that those closest to me knew was inevitable. After an afternoon at Burke Williams Day Spa I returned home and immediately felt the knots form in my back, neck, and stomach.

I want to be very clear about this. My husband never asked me to clean like a mad woman, or cook every night. In fact, he is the primary cook in our home. My children never asked me to do anything outside of love and feed them. My friends stopped offering help because I always denied it. "I've got it," "I am going to slow down next week," "No I don't need anything, I am Superwoman!"

The reality is I am not a perfectionist. I am afraid that I am not enough. I am afraid that what is in me to give will not measure up to the invisible yard stick we mothers, wives, and women, line up against every morning, and every night. I am afraid to be fierce, powerful, sexy, and flawed. Afraid that other women won't befriend me and men will find me intimidating. So I run a doomed obstacle course that I carefully set up for myself every time I am afraid to accept my shine, but not anymore.

 Today I allot ten minutes just to pose in sexy underwear that used to be reserved for special occasions. I invest thirty minutes every morning and every evening to surround myself in aroma therapeutic showers, and I don't apologize for it. I don't apologize for being big, for being destined, for being a star even when I try not to shine. Today, I am the woman my husband saw at the end of a rose covered aisle. And I am growing bigger, and brighter by the moment.

TO BEGIN WITH
Eboni

To begin with...

I am an illusionist,
in love with a disappearing act stolen straight from
the fingers of Houdini.
Open my hands/Close my eyes
Turned a man of water into vapor
then allowed this condensation to drown my memories.

I release like the breath to make inhalation possible.

We won't pretend.
You were never mine.
You belonged to red earth,

The clink of hard liquor at the bottom of an empty belly,
The giggles of girls in corners waiting for me to turn my back,

Let's not be selfish.
Your wings are dry.
You never were mine.
I love you
   (You will never know...)

I love you
   (...the sweat)
I love you
   (...the shit I trudge through daily)

Abracadabra

My phone remains silent.
I avoid email because I'm developing a rejection complex.
Find myself typing thoughts I should keep to myself.
Hoping you'll remember.
Knowing it's unlikely.
My fist loosens
      Nothing else matters
I won't betray who I am
even if   I don't know what   that is.
No more chasing rainbows,
Waiting for rain then lighting flame to my eyelashes

I am insecure and too young to be sexy.
I am the little girl hiding in the closet ribs showing.
The man I love is as good as smoke and mirrors.
And I have resolved to her kissing you goodnight,

But when you close your eyes,
I'll be there, waiting for the car with the gash in its side,

Skin wearing new scars and tattoos.
My thighs wound around your waist;
nails digging tunnels into your shoulder blades;
Tears painting rivers in your cheekbones.

You will wake to a watery shadow on your ceiling,
A poem and a sky blue ribbon sitting under your tongue.

But I will have evaporated.

This heathen cannot pray another prayer or heaven
may come crashing down on her head.

Maybe this time you will hear me.
Maybe I don't exist.
Maybe I'm an escape artist or just an illusionist.
I forget.
You were really never mine
to begin with.

Sister SOS *(Inspired by Kathleen Cleaver)*
nikki skies

She's heard more eulogies than poetry so I wrote this for her.
Amidst the sips of licorice tea, I asked her
"what she would do differently."

She replied she'd "love as fearlessly as she fought
take more time,
soak the greens instead of rinse 'em"
research his heart as she did antiquity.

She truly believed that for years she had a melody
but never a song
no vibration
no balance
"conquer your soul's duality" she told me
the world is depending on you to love
surrender, Sister.

History Lesson

Amanda Johnston

On the day when she asks
where her father went
      I will not mention the junkies
who called him into the night
or the round willing women
who warmed his rolling bed
or how he could have run
in Tennessee for the University
on scholarship.
      I will not mention my husband
the father she has now
who doesn't own her last name
but knows she loves ripped jeans
who her friends are
and how to make her smile
when the endless corners of temptation
call her into the dark.
      I will not go to the forked road,
a choice between reality and fantasy,
but I will tell her a story about a gift
born to a false prophet who lived
despite the salted ground.

Over Breakfast
Amanda Johnston

While passing milk
and bowls of Cheerios,
I spoon-feed discussion
down her throat; at eight,
she already ignores me.

Do you know what a period is?

I casually ask like I'm proofing
her papers unaware of her
ample hips, hairy legs, round breasts.

She wobbles her head side-to-side
deflecting the question with concrete ears.
I force another spoonful.

One day you will begin to bleed
down there.

The words cut her further from me
slicing at the last bit of flesh
that separates our girl/woman roles.

vagina

menstruation

sex

Deeper the knife passes.

These words fall from my quivering lips

like bombs over her "I love first grade" T-shirt.

She swallows the milk hard,

keeps her face low,

asks if she can add strawberries

like they do on TV.

Teacup

April Jones

Hearts are not made for this.
They are not developed inside intricate cages to be plucked and hung on some dirty, spray-painted soapbox.

My teacup, a bodyguard from a heated wake up call, sat on the edge of the coffee table we found by the roadside. I watched it hold onto the boil, fury seething in its hollow.
The steam loomed over the liquid surface, waiting for its reflection to appear.

My breath clung to a moment, flimsy pulp and sting, while my body housed a fire in my chest.
Porcelain is not built to support the explosion of failure. The seething in my lungs, desperate for release.

If I were a teacup you could hold me to your lips, careful of the potential sting.
I would know how to exhume the roar of my insides- cautious, we understand how this works. You wait for cool down. You test with a simple placement of mouth.

I miss the quiet between us.
We don't speak to each other anymore and it makes my skin hang like a dress I will never fit into.
You cannot read the rodeo in my eyes, the lack of sleep beneath them, the dark moon that sits on my head like a plum stained crown since we last fought.

This morning a sunbeam reached my body while I slept.
I let myself pretend it was your hand gliding along my spine, a low flying airplane.

Brave adventurer, you found domicile in the collapsed dune of my back.

Silly Island did not recognize the selfishness in a search like that.

How it still offers itself up, an obsequious display, cheapened with every finger you push through its soft surfaces. Testing the readiness of skin and muscle you never had a palate for.

When I got up this morning, I thought of the women who inspire you now. I see them combing their perfect hair, into foolproof side ponytails with smiles the size of my regret- Their matched puzzle piece sparkle, how they rise out of bed angels.

I went to the bathroom, scrubbed the blood and make up from my eyes, hovering an inch from the mirror for hours. All figure of breath and steam, holding amazingly still, waiting for my reflection.

exhale

jeanann verlee

fingers are roadmaps
private journals
poems written on the edges of hands
fingers are thick or long, fine, fat, scarred, arthritic
sometimes even missing

and how does a woman feel
in the weight of 40 fingers
8 arms
3 hours

40 fingers that grasp and prod
lift unzip unbuckle
falling boots echo against hardwood floors
> *Please don't hurt my dog.*

and how does a woman feel
in the heat of 40 fingers
folding over breasts, between thighs
every thrust. cut. blooded with laughter
every, "Suck it bitch."
grunting sweat drips into burning eyes, crosses lips
a salt that cannot be washed away
> *Guys stop. Please. We're friends. Don't do this to me.*

and a detour through Jersey City – from Midtown – to get to the

Bronx

made perfect sense after 3 glasses of wine, 6 shots of Hennessey

and uncounted beers

a game of head-to-head, drink-for-drink

a game she didn't think she could lose

just like it made perfect sense for everyone in the car to walk the lady to the door

perfect sense that they all had to take a piss

made sense when they all asked for another beer

and it almost even made sense when someone started kissing her neck

from the open refrigerator door

now cloaked in these demons,

she brands herself a whore

you see, mind replaces memory with what you can handle

like peering through the grey haze of day-after contact lenses

blurred faces, chests, nipples, fingers inside

chunks of time absent

miniature black holes

pink pencil nub erasers rubbing holes through white paper

leaving the tiniest of lead marks for the memory to retrace

or reinvent

this lifetime of fists and black gravel

home-schooled on Budweiser flashcards and back-alley couches

commemoration medals tattooed for each sin survived

but even *this* lifetime cannot fight off 40 fingers –
can only survive them
so, swallow tears, keep eyes on the ceiling
don't think how you used to fuck your husband here
don't panic – you *can* survive this

skin pulled tight, stretching, swelling
the inner body furious to outgrow itself, to escape
to tear flesh, leap from the bed
race the stairs
find a cop
or a gun
    Please, just don't hurt my dog.
and her relief in black laced thigh highs and shaved pussy
they are unarmed, cannot mock her later for being
unsexy

but for now she is a slut
a host, inviting, serving, asking for more
"You want me, don't you, baby."
between lovers, her cells seize with shock and exhaustion
they slap and punch, fuck her back in to consciousness
more cock and tongue than any rag doll was made to withstand
they tear at her between sharpened teeth
seams shredded, puss and Polyfil fibers spilling out
soon she'll be tossed aside

the broken doll at the bottom of the toy chest

naked at dawn
her fingers trace the furniture, the walls,
the refrigerator door
floorboards moan under brittle, pacing toes
cradling souvenirs of bruises and dried blood
she is torn, still screaming between her thighs
she makes the bed
walks the dog

and how does a woman feel
limp drunk
in the shame of 40 fingers
8 arms
3 hours
the words drip silently from closed lips
after four years of denial –
    exhale
the shame is not ours to hold
anymore

time line
abena koomson

1974
The girl born on Tuesday
came out smelling like black funk

birthed by the soulfinger
that slaps the flat key
of a brass horn

& the left platform shoe
that didn't make it back from the disco
call the Kwame Kum & Efua Amofua

Daddy & Mommy
They were meant for each other
And here comes Tuesday's girl

Slope of mouth: shape of Ghanaian coastline
Sound of words: Connecticut concrete
This same mouth

kissed by a girl
too soon to know

how tiny hands stroke a face

or fondle an ear
in the cracked basement
of a Hartford high rise

We found music in
our mothers hollering us home
the tight afro of a boy named Michael

In 1982
when Stevie was Ebony
and Paul was Ivory

Tuesday's girl was a negro song
The split backbone of a red hymnal
The weeping palm of prayer

The bony legs that dangled
From the pews of the North United Methodist Church
Where the *Holy Ghost spirit is movin' just like a magnet*

In 1984
Jesus was the crisp staccato
on the tongues of swaying worshippers

Penmanship Books

Jesus was the squeeze of your mother's hand
while on your knees
where you soften your tears to hear her

The year Challenger punctured the sky
Tuesday's girl read a chapter
in the book called America
The one God folded
but has yet to come back to
A journal whose pages were torn

burned
hung
and whipped

fibers pressed from the pine
we so proudly hailed
to the pulp of blood bone and chains

that sleep beneath the Atlantic
the Connecticut
and the Mississippi

In the summer of '91
Tuesday's girl found poetry
wrote it down in lover as journal

in journal as empty husk of corn
She smelled like paper birch
but no trees recognized her scent

In 1995 she finds love in search of home
He was a crackle of love laughter
she, a bent branch no leaves left

By the time the towers crash into her city
Tuesday's girl is a naked whisper,
a breeze on the urban coastline

One year later
Tuesday's girl returns
to the land of the mother
she names herself *I*
claims the open mouthed syllable
for her own tongue

I woke up every 5am
to a laughing chorus
of roosters and yard dogs

I called out to the women
selling waakye and dried fish at dawn
who sang the sun into rising

Penmanship Books

I am not paper birch
I am Kum tree
the seed of my name

Accra sun makes me the color of palm oil
as bright as fufu in abenkwan
as large as Arhin teeth

I am from the 104 year old grandma
who thought Ben Gay was toothpaste
and lives to laugh about it

My hands
her hands
gather in the same bowl
These autumn feet
These kpanlogo hips
this rise of cheek
this clench of fist
this coastline spread of lips

all know
how to say
my name.

SUN/RISE
Ebele Ajogbe

Me and the sun
we know what it's like
to wake up
when the whole world's still sleeping
when your lover's still sleeping
in your arms

'cos the gods leant me
a spoonful of sugar
in the shape of the woman
laying beside me
Her sweet honeysuckle breath
caressing my face
each time she exhales

My queen sleeps…
but I know her spirit
is awake
and she can see me
watching her - intently

I can't help it:
my soul plays jazz melodies
on her skin

and she wakes…

She wakes from her feline slumber
and we rise
and fall
and sing

Yes we rise
and fall
and sing

Inhibitions lost
boundaries long surpassed
we rise and fall
and sing our bodies
with sweet violence…

MY NAME IS NKIRU

Ebele Ajogbe

Aunty, I promise I'll do my homewok
I'll wash my pant & uniform everydey
I'll fetch wota every mornin
I'll stop playin wit boyz
I'll sit wit my legz clozed
I'll always greet Uncle Ajayi
I won't wet my bed
I'll stop aksin stupid questionz…

She said it woz for my own good
dey were preparin me for de future
or else no-one wud want me
and I'd bring shame to de whole familee
and I'd die a spinsta
and de whole village wud laff at me

but I promise I'll do my homewok /I'll wash my pant & uniform everyday/I'll fetch wota every morning/I'll stop playin wit boyz I'll sit wit my legz…
 dey held me down de way dey held mommy down
when she was givin birth to my little broddah
 de Coke bottle laid brokin on de floor…
it felt like somebodi jus put hot pepper in my private part
de glass…felt like hot pepper down der OOOOOOH
Aunty, I promise I'll fetch wota every …EEEEEEEHHH
I'll stop playin wit boyz, AUNTY
AUNTY, I'll stop playin wit boyz
I'll sit wit my legz   AUNTY I'M DYING OOOOOOH
AUNTY, AUNTY I'll alwayz greet Uncle
I won't wet my bed
I'll stop aksin stupid YEEEEEEEEEEYI
YEY, YEY, YEY, YEY, YEEEEEEEEEEEEEEYI
I DEY DIE OOOOOOOOH,
AUNTY, YEEEEEEEEEEEEEEYI……

Rosewater Perfume

Lynne Procope

The woman across from me
on the 12:08 train to the edge of the world
wears a smile that says she knows, I
can smell it on her
and it's not the fresh scent of fuck
or at least not of the kind of sex so sweet you
wake up in the throes of it all week, wear it
home to a single bed or keep as a memento
of the insides of your lover's body. This isn't
the type of musk that hugs your memory or makes
you sway at the elevator to an internal music.

It's something so stale it'd died in the body before hers
and poured out only from spite. Her boyfriend
hasn't loved his wife in years. In fact he hates her
enough to screw this one twice on Monday nights,
despite the highlights gone to brass, the pancake paint,
the bitter jaw and mean eyes, despite
the three day old black and blue, another man's mark
turning on her thigh. He gets with her
on Mondays and keeps her till the last train. He pulls
her back to wallow in the front seat of his wife's
pretty German car, despite the fact
we all know the mark on her; it's not his mark
and the smell's not just his cruelty alone.

And isn't that the point, that with all the wear
and the monopoly of ruin, women like this one
own the body more than girls like me ever can
with our practiced agendas and careful meals,
our multi-love feminism that lets us fall
so perfectly apart in the absence of what
we bargain for with such care. We collapse
without the benefit of bruises, implode too neatly,

our argument and our pride in tact. But this

Long Island rose is nodding on the Far Rock train,
grateful for midnight and its benign reconciliations,
for the luxury of cab fare from the station. Rose knows
she's grown faded but the parts she brought are the parts
she owns. She knows that all we save is left for rot,
- so use it.

She counts the value of a body in the shades
of its paint, the stale drift of its borrowed
perfume, in the two beers he bought before pulling
down the pants his wife put out the night before.

Two Sundays from now, parked
on the South Conduit, caught in church traffic
or an IKEA snarl on Kennedy Blvd, he'll sit
quietly beside his wife, her two carat diamond,
limp on his right thigh, his eyes glancing
on their sons, theirs glazed over at a DVD
of something educational to subdue their natural
twitching. He'll catch the scent of all his sweet
breaking apart into rot and its individual slivers
will each carry a salty eau de toilet. He'll think,
ah god and nothing else.

For a minute you see he was simply unholy, for a
moment worth noticing and keeping apart and she
was the sty in his blind forgiveness. Against the best
advice he'll wish for his Rose, plan on a Monday
which must come before the end of the earth because Rose
resurrects his dismal survival, she convinces

with what she gathers in the mouth.

Penmanship Books

The Trome l'oeil Anna Nicole
Lynne Procope

the secret is
there are no movable parts anymore.
lift up my layers, i'm not a real girl,
just a scarecrow to warn your daughters,
melted frame for fields of flash bulbs.

there's a fever of grief under
the woman you imagined as me.
unexpected, the mouth hidden
under vamp and giggle, the edge,
its ragged cuts smoothed beneath
a soft light. it seems we all bleed to feel.
there's just the question of
who inflicts the wound.

i say mourn for women like me.
i say take regrets over empty.   thirty nine
is an awful age to die but i was
too full of wants. i coveted
the all you've got, perfect boundaries,
damp pillows, mend and tear.
and all along i was a want myself, a thing
coveted and kept.

but i tell you this, if you whisper,
throat cut to a coo, if you play desire
as love they'll want to love you or
want to stay the night and you learn
to split the difference, to hedge the bet
in numbers. i'll tell you too

that the old man loved me
this full sweet mouth, swell breast, crucial
curve of hip and ass.   i made
the dead guess at my natural color,
i could complicate a situation by entering the room.
he had to have me. and i deserved

what i got for what i took and
what was taken from me. i survived

sucker punches to the womb, you do not know
how tough i am, can't count the hard strikes
against me, you- won't even swallow for love,
won't put your hand on your man cause he
didn't take out the trash.

but i knew trash, what was cast off
and could not be kept. i wanted only
a little for myself. what you keep is all

you are and i can only keep this up
but so long before this body wears down
and gives up its secret. i am a mystery
of hot sorrows, a tight red dress worn
to hide what slips away underneath.
the dress like the body is a prison.

so call me dorothy with red shoes
and pill box, norma jean with portrait of new
man, call me billie, voice breaking down
like ore to rust , call me woman in portrait
without eyelids or fear. the name's vikie lynn,
i'm a texas girl gone bad, i'm a mother
with a history
of dancing on tables. here's my pretty

pink heart all wet and ready, the failure,
the throb. did you think that i wanted to grow old,
to spread and fade, lose my tongue
to your spotlight,
my heart to the promises of fools?

Flectere: (*latin: to bend*)
Lynne Procope

Bend, disclose the lie you
are telling you are orchid
lip breakable, too much
to touch, you are mauve,
mourning cloth, unarmored,
unlikely, impossible

fully believed in and you
are at your last shade of bruise,
so accord a tone, flat, barge
drawn as breath to the depth of
your bed, sing, regard the empty
miss him, even in other men's
hands, watch the hours once
so full explode into rippled
distance and bend-
the first lie was,
go, I will not miss you.
the second his act of
contrition, the third:
this reconciliation. Declare
a holiday from his wide mouth
from the soft sulcus where his

hand defined your spine as
organ, demand room to dredge
breath, and scream.

Listen for the echo hint at the
edge of your abyss. Sidestep
the gap, give him back his
sparrow, grieve for what you
gave, weep for the raw, wail
for the armor-

How are you so soft shelled
and still walking? You,
will agree to supervised visits,
see him only in mixed company
burn the love letters, lie-
of course I'll still love you.

And bend, he is not the
honey or the bread. sing,
he is not the miracle of wine.

Testify only to the blessed,
the prism light, force of dew,
electric memory of rooftops,
hubris of, *I should never have*

forgiven you.
Forgiving is your blessing,
forgetting a soft luxury on
your tongue. When you
crack invisible, leak light
pour your shadow into
the side stepped abyss
learn how to tell time
truthfully, you are- half
past dissolve, eighteen
minutes to becoming,
straight up on the witching
hour of woman.

and bend- then rage because
this- is not kind, rage
because you become
an animal tracking
your own disaster, incant
these wild totems of your
specific creation until this
world breaks itself down
to fit you.

Folded & Shoved
Nicole Homer

How unfair it was of god
 to shove everything inside of women
  (EVERYTHING)

How many times did he fold the feelings
 how many creases did he put in life
   before it would fit
& what did he add to it
  so it would dissolve and not dissolve
 in blood
   (& tears)
& how much did every women get
  that it can leak out
        crawl out
          fumble out
and there is always more?
Why, god,
   does lust become a bruise
       which swells and turns blue?
and would you know

Would you know you wanted me
 if your cock were not hard

    and telling you,
           would you know?
  if you wanted me
 if your dick was limp
if everything were folded so small
   & shoved somewhere inside of you
     would you still know
& would there always be more?
enough for blood
enough for tears
always more,
        always more

How unfair that god
   shoved everything inside
and so ineffectively
 that it will not even stay there
   & escapes as blood,
 or more often, tears

I would know i wanted you
   even if my desire for you
      was not hot
and dripping down my leg

16

Crystal Senter Brown

black biker shorts
2 sizes too small
oversized Cross Colors t-shirt, doubled up socks, pink
Reeboks
hair to my waist, braided, dusty from
long days spent at the dollar pool
skin slick from cocoa butter
mouth sweetened with jolly ranchers

we tumble out our bedroom window into the bushes
boys from 3 blocks away meet us
carrying bagged bottles of Boones Farm
the cute one with the curly hair says I'm pretty
his freckles make me dizzy

16 finds me
very much still a country girl,
loving Michael Jackson and Slick Rick
my sister and I run wild
sneaking back in before daddy comes home
from the night shift

On his mother's bed

Crystal Senter Brown

hall pass crumpled on shag carpeting
ripped jeans tossed aside
knees wide apart
air smells like sweat/ youth
cheap perfume and laffy taffy
he is experienced…I pretend to be
he pushes
struggles, tears
hurts, tears stream
and pool on my right cheek

his Mother will be home soon
I will be late for 7th period

he hands me my jeans and
my teenage girl underwear
cotton, blue polka dots, granny-cut

we skip across the highway
hand in hand
armed with band instruments and backpacks
we are young
for now…

Serpents & Stepmothers
Genevieve Van Cleve

Snow White, Cinderella and my stepsons have something in common. A wicked stepmother.

Now I haven't forced those boys to rely on a magic rat and a pumpkin for transportation to school events. And I haven't gone down to the junior high with a cape and a sackful of poisonous apples. Here kid, want an apple? But I have made them do their homework because I am that evil old crone that makes them dinner every other week.

(Cackle Loudly For Really Long Time).

Let me just say I have no idea what I'm doing. They are boys. I am not. They make swords out of everything. Make up kung fu moves called Fists of Fury. And they eat like a puma, neck deep in a mostly dead antelope. It's very, very disturbing.

I'm terrified that the only conversation they'll have with a college girl in a bar is how they can never really love because their stepmother ruined their life.

My role as a step parent breaks down into the romantic

conflict in the Sound of Music. Either I'm Baroness
Von Ebberfield with a diamond studded turban and
Diamond covered vagina, convincing Captain Von Trapp to send
his children to live in the forest with wolves. OR I'm
that maniacally perky Maria making lederhosen out of
curtains and secretly considering divorcing Christ for
an even more demanding man.

While I haven't worked out my personal parental style
I promise you children that I will never force you to
sing folk songs in front of the other villagers. Folk
music is obnoxious and irritating. We'll make up our
own songs as we trudge over the Adolescent Alps into
Very Grown Up Valley

The hills are alive and they're eating people fa la
la la (Sing it like Ozzy).

I'm dispensing advice like a woman with a closet full
of sweater sets. But instead of little kitties battin'
yarn, my sweaters are covered with protest signs,
poets, and pro-choice buttons.

I hope they get it. I hope they get that I love them.
I don't care if I wasn't there for their conception. I
tuck them in at night. And I remember. Even after 30

years, there is still a tiny part of me that wants my
mom and dad to get back together. I get it.

I Googled stepmother and found the quote, "Better to
survive a serpent than a stepmother." And maybe that's
true. Maybe that true.

But like I always tell them as I deliver platter after
platter of liver and onions to the table that they'll
have to finish before I make them go out and farm in the dark
…Children, children these are the memories that
will keep future therapists on their toes. That's why
your father married me!

Now, who wants pie?

miss carol's house

Imani Tolliver

  sits tall on the bayou
  there are imposing metal stairs
  that climb into an impossible rush
  the pounding
  that makes the veal thin, thin
  the laughter and stories
  the ones that come during the holidays

      you remember dat lime green bikini i had
      member mawma
      yeah, it was hang ten
      wit da feet on the side
      yeah, daddy said if he caught me in dat again
      he'd whoop my ass good

now, all miss carol's babies is loud
but sherry's bray stands above all
beatin da meat
into a mash
proud of her accomplishment
she holds it up

      lookit

Penmanship Books

    yeah, dat how ya do it

the accent here
stews a bit
with the tongue of the eastern shore
there ain't no regular southern twang in these parts

sherry's brother-in-law
pickled slowly, sitting along side of us
at the round kitchen table
it worked this way
 miss carol circled round while
sherry's brother
cut the fat and gristle from the flesh
passing it to his right
to a visitor, like me
to pound it thin and tender
then, we slid margarine on the belly of each ribbon
breaded it with crumbs
parsley and romano cheese and rolled
it into a tight, tiny cigar
the size a lady might smoke
on the pan it goes, packed tight
miss carol inspects it
gives it a bit of olive oil
and in the oven it goes at 350°

for how long i ask

>   till you can smell it real good
>   ya pull one out and if it is tender
>   ya know it's done

miss carol's husband had open-heart surgery
and has a spot on his lung
two centimeters

>   he could be buried on that recliner
>   he tells me i can't handle dis house
>   but i wanna show him that i can

out my name
Imani Tolliver

when he called me nigger last night
over the food i cooked for him
with herbs i sang to on sunday mornings
a cup of dark coffee in one hand, a cigarette in the other

when he called me nigger
i thought about all the dances with him

celia cruz and the wet spring grass of the capitol
my friends wondered who this brother was
touching me that way and holding my hand
saying sweet things about new friendships
on porch steps late at night

when he called me nigger the way he did
with his regular friends
the ones who grandma would approve of
lawyers and light girls with long, straightened hair
good over thanksgiving
with the daddy he calls sir
and the mama he calls everyday

when he said that word

i thought of plantations
and hanged negroes, black as cain

i thought i gangsters in l.a.
as their hands signal the hieroglyph
of brotherhood, death and revenge
street and good times
watching the backs of your brothers
who know you as family
under streetlights and bouncing cars

i remember late nights with girlfriends
inking the receiver with talks of the gone wrong brothers
you know how they be girl, they all the same

i never once thought of my mother and her jesus
moaning a requiem i never understood
or my father, who taught me to pull eggplants
to love books and expect little from men, from himself

i never thought of my brother
once a child i changed, a crip i cursed
now giving praises on a rug i bought on crenshaw boulevard

that word never felt right in my mouth
but i used it just the same

when it came down to insulting brothers just the right way
to remind them that they were nothing
not even a name

when i told him all this
asked for an apology
and told him to talk to me like his mama or older sis
he said

    do not expect that kind of respect
    you're one of my boys
    girl, you my nigga

ode

Imani Tolliver

if the only definition of love
lies in its in articulation
let us never speak its truth
and be pulled with its heat between

let us moan a requiem of a past
and dream a new world
one and many

if love lies truly in its in articulation
than i will never speak it
and let its heat ember in my bones
and let its hot trickle
lick delicious across my skin

if love has no mouth
only metaphor and the space before speaking it
let it rest in my mouth
and i will hold its muscle soft in my jaws
pinking it with the blood
that holds my thighs full
that feeds my body when moons shine brightest
if love has no internal voice

let its music swim cacophonous and melodic in me

if i give this to you
oh, burning wood
oh, red and blue soft stone
if i put it in your mouth
from mine

will you cup it in your hands
palm it over your aching parts
your knees from praying
your eyes from crying
your belly from its bleed

if love's only word
is its inarticulate whisper
its sound smooth as a lick on polished wood
its color darker than countries

hear my lament
darker and more silent

listen
       listen

take

       listen

return
       whisper

wait

say
       say nothing

i

hold your heart to my skin

wait
       whisper

hum

       hum

defending frida

Imani Tolliver

i don't know why she is popular with other people but i will tell you why i love
frida

despite a famous husband she, supportive in a rebozo and garden flowers in her hair,
  painted
despite the judas body,
  she painted

  the body that cut their son in pieces, no glory
just pieces of a boy
and still she painted

her diego
found the flesh of women irresistible
as did she
the sweet of it
irresistible

i wonder what touching frida would be like
if you were her lover
would you caution the seams
the cut and sewn parts

would she hold the meat of you
in the same mouth warmed by posole, chili

would her lick be soft as a sliver of flan
with caramel at the tip
or would you have to coax the sweet
peel back the bristle
like the brutal, but succulent agave
to find the tender meat waiting
supple, warm
becoming the taste of what tastes it

i have so much to judge myself by
how much i exercise
what i weigh
whether i eat meat, enough vegetables
were they organic
were they justly farmed
did i keep my tongue in heaven today
am i telling the truth
  am i being responsible
  authentic
  true

i never knew frida
but her paintings follow me

Penmanship Books

they come as cards, trinkets
from women, always
from my mother, mostly

and the jewelry
the paintings
the tiny altars
the boxes and books

tell me
speak
you must speak
cough the ribbons of your tongue free
lick the flesh that calls you
ink your fingertips when you cannot find a brush
find walls when canvas is not nearby
love hard and mighty
put flowers in your hair
the big, gorgeous ones from your garden
wear the colors of your own flag
create when baffled
create when sorrowful. afraid. brave. brilliant.

abandon the prickle of fear
and be of your own making
begin from deep, deep

feel the tremor
the push, the work root
the quaking blossom
of who you really are

let light
let you
be free

Harlem's Photograph (or why I look at you that way)
Kimberley Taylor

last time I saw you
I peeled the truth from your skin
layers of passion, glossy
immortalize you.

bewildered,
I am paralyzed by your charm
transfixed by your light

you continue to baffle me

the memories trick me
divine imitations of love
blend, meld, merge,

let me look at you again.
overwhelm my pupils
you, beautiful muse
stain my journal
listen to my heart beat sketch divine manifestations
in the shape of your eyes

I will fall upon your lips and become reality
I will shade your outline with obscure worries,
then walk your footsteps through the shadows of my mind

meet me there....

and we will hold hands
dance our fingertips to a melody of
murmuring heartbeats
and our smiles will amplify our silence.

damn, where did you come from?

basic black and white captured
in the sculpture of my heart
frozen in time,
the rhythm of your absence echoes
the beat of your sigh

you leave me breathless
spellbound at every glance
your photograph,
the last time, I swore I
could taste the breeze of your kiss
and smell you in my dreams

I long for Harlem.

A Persian Gulf War Love Story
Courtenay Aja Barton

But you,
you were my first kiss and,
shortly thereafter,
my first fistfight –
back before I knew how to spell love.
I remember
back before Dennis got sent upstate and
Gordy got shot.
Yellow ribbons everywhere swaying in
the autumn's honest air,

I was too shy not to hold your hand and
we watched
as the army tanks rolled down Jefferson,
when I learned how to spell war,
which I learned how to spell before love.

But you,
you caught me by surprise
underneath the cherry tree,
the cherry tree that grew the red red cherries.
You are so
Perfect.

His Rib: Stories, Poems & Essays by Her

First Apartment Poem

Courtenay Aja Barton

You own 53 pairs of shoes and a solitary fork.

You have yet to framed that 160,000 $ Ivy League degree in a 200 $ frame

and then find out your boss's nanny (high school drop out) gets paid more than you do.

You have considered selling your possessions to pay rent

but you have no possessions (save books, and you will not part with them)

You consider selling yourself. Closed, invitation-only auction.

Instead of selling yourself, you write a poem.

You send that poem to several a literary magazine.

You love your poem. You wonder how this poem could

not be published. It cannot not be published.

You do not receive any rejection letters.

You do not receive any acceptance letters.

You go back to work and thank divinity your benefits are good

because they are paying for your therapist.

With overtime, you make ends meet. Life

is disappointing. You are disappointed.

Of course, having grown up in the ghetto,

you should have known life would be such.

Hard. But you have been that smart girl everyone said

would surely be successful. In fact, your salary

is 10,000 less than the tuition your scholar benefactor used to pay

to that Ivy Tower. You can't sleep.
Your therapist won't give you antidepressants.
Your internist won't give you antidepressants.
You sleep all the time whenever at home because you don't
own a chair to sit upon. You only just have your bed and it
is very seductive. Rent is late. You cry.
Then, despite the ample seductive qualities of your bed
you cannot sleep without drinking a cup of
Benadryl. So you drink cups of Benadryl.

And you would never complain. Because you are black
and a woman and did not grow up monied.
You've rubbed shoulders with the monied,
and of course you are smart, so you still feel
entitled, but you are not. But you don't complain because
soldiers are dying in a war they'd rather not fight,
police encamp around your block, a baby
dies of AIDS somewhere, a father loses the job that feeds his kids,
a woman is raped. And all you are is empty
in your empty first apartment.

I Live Alone
Tamara Blue

I bake cookies in the middle of the night

Not because I'm hungry.

I just really like the smell of cookies, when I'm sleeping.

It makes the house warm and cozy .

I live alone ,

Smoke in the restroom,

Cook with no top on,

Air dry after a shower

For hours if I want to.

Do laundry at 2 in the morning on a Wednesday.

I have fashion shows and photo shoots all by myself.

Computer in the hallway, hair dryer is in the living room, condoms in the bathroom, candles in the kitchen…

I put things where I want them.

And they stay there.

My fridge has vodka and salad.

A chicken breast from weeks ago,

My dishes stay dirty and I don't mind.

30 years old and I live alone,

No children,

No husband

And right now, I wouldn't have it any other way.

The smell of sugar cookies at 3 am is soothing.
It's the part of home you miss when you move out,
The love you need when your bed is empty
And your sheets are cold, the blanket still smells like my most recent ex-lover,
Or so he was called.

I never realized how often I would snuggle my head into
the bend of his neck and shoulder.
Rest the weight of his grown man on top of me.
Wrap the strength of his arms around me.

He never loved me...
Just loved my cookie: warm and sweet,
      Real good ...
Too sweet for his baby teeth
So I learned to keep my cookies to myself
And my house always smells

Like fresh baked cookies.

Requiem para los Orishas

Gabriela Garcia Medina

Oshun fertiliza corazones
Y Yemaya moves oceans
Shango's fire burns in constant motion
Y el viento blows in devotion of
Oya
playing tricks on
Ellegua
clearing the path for
Obbatala
Orula envelops almas viejas
Y las manda al mas alla
As I light a candle
Por los Dioses de Iffa
And pray that they will live through me
That their energies will consume me
Dioses Lucumi, Dioses Yoruba
Rooted in Africa, planted in Cuba
Persisting Traditions
Cuando me sube el Santo
I live in their visions
Experience the Supreme
Through lucid dreams
Que me muestran la verdad absoluta

And though I would like to invoke their holistic presence
My spirit goes to war with my existing reality
Attaches itself to the physical/Ignoring the spiritual
Atrapando mi alma en un mundo material
Que se pierde en un abismo espiral
Until Oshun's golden rays are too far away to reach me
Until Yemaya's oceans turn to deserts of sand
Until Ellegua no longer holds out his hand
To show me a path clear of bricks and stones
And Shango's fire no longer makes its home
Inside these bones to feed my passions
So I spit on my ancestors
Label their traditions "old fashioned"
And try to survive on my own, void of substance
Because all their "folk tales" and "superstitions"
Become nothing but distractions and contradictions
I lose my spirit
Until I can no longer hear it
It becomes numb until I can't feel it
These times we are living in war
We embrace the idea of another God
A God who's divinations
Are founded on the occupation
Of indigenous nations
A God that serves as justification
For murder in the name of liberation

Un Dios que crece a causa del sufrimiento de nuestra gente
Un Dios que miente
Y no se arrepiente
Un Dios que vive en la miseria de pobres inocentes
Un Dios que no tiene nombre
Y abusa de la bondad de nuestros hombres
Y el amor de nuestras mujeres
Un Dios que no muere
Because he exists only in fear
    A God who's Oshun is money instead of honey
Who's Yemaya no es vida pero es muerte
Who's Ellegua is the law that clears the path for greed
And who's Shango is the fire of a gunshot
Aimed at the father of a son of a family in need
A God who's blessings can be bought and sold
If his battles are fought and won
Who's words are taught to young impressionable minds
Disguised as honor and patriotism
Meanwhile our people are dying for a nationalism
That doesn't represent them
That doesn't defend them
Yet they die to become heroes for the same God condemns them
and makes us forget

Where we came from.

Penmanship Books

4 Womyn

Gabriela Garcia Medina

He was the illest M.C.
So I took home the CD
He .Was. My. First.
Every   Time
His hand hit my face
Replaced and embrace with a Beat
Boxing was his strength
Said he was born
With the gift
But he promised to resist
Raising his fist at me again
Said the bruising would heal and I would feel better tomorrow
Once the swelling disappeared
Said he'd write me a poem so sincere
About how beautiful I was
And with word of regret
He would write that poem
That made me forget
His hooks were a threat
I succumbed to in denial
And I lost consciousness when he battled me in freestyle

(an excerpt from the poem 4 Womyn)

bittersweet

Erica S. Kamara

in Monrovia
25 years, tomorrow
i will be born unto an uppity, blunt, and giving woman
with thin patience
and Liberia in her swagger
i will be born unto a soft spoken, unrighteous Sierra Leonean man
with thick lips, and Creole in his hum
God would later ordain him as preacher
they will stay together for such a short time after my birth
that the sudden break-up would later induce me to believe
their sole purpose for meeting was to conceive me
and thrust me into this living
he will leave my mother long before
he leaves for America when I turn four
his leaving would make her clutch to me
her clutching would cause me to sour
my sourness will turn into unfeeling wrath
when I meet him again at 13

   later, without knowing it, he will teach me about forgiveness
   long before he comes to accept his responsibility as father
   some time after, he will grow to become a good friend
   and she and I will mature to have an understanding

too difficult for words

i will love her for all that she has not grown to love about herself

and become the daughter-friend whom she consults for wisdom and prayer

the three of us will say so much to one another

in our silence

but they would never figure out why he left

why she clutched and controlled

why I became numb, retreated and wrote

but through it all

i would come into flower

a ripening, ever-evolving

resilient woman

fists pumping high

when I turn 25

tomorrow

i

will

be

reborn.

His Rib: Stories, Poems & Essays by Her

Rumors of War: A Memoir
Erica Kamara

Pow. Pow.

The sound of gunshots lingers in the evening air. Inside, we immediately take cover after peeking out to inquire about the gunfire. It is in our front yard. Two men, clothed in dirty denim jeans, wearing red bandannas on their heads, are flaunting their guns as they run toward the pathway leading to our front door.

We lay low. I press my body hard onto the tan bedroom rug, wishing I could dissolve into the floor. I am terrified.

It is mid-1990, on a quiet Sunday in Liberia. I am at home with Mama, my two adolescent sisters and my one-year-old brother. My other sister is away visiting with friends. Today, we are enjoying the company of a few other relatives who live with us. Earlier, the government issued a warning for everyone to stay at home, so we have been lounging around the house all day. My nine-year-old mind does not understand fully, but I know in my gut that it's a serious mandate.

"Everyone in the house come outside now and line up," shouts one of the men in demanding tone, leaving us all frantic.

"Come outside or we'll kill you," the other voice emerges as he fires another shot to emphasize that we should hurry. Our actions are as scattered as our minds. Their voices grow louder as we rumble, trying to figure out what to do.

"Shhh ... Don't make any noise," Mama preps us, making eye contact with each person.

"When we go out there, just do what they tell you," she whispers. No one responds with words. Our eyes tell her we understand.

On her inside she is shaken but does not want us to take notice. Mama has always been the rock of our family. She is the super single mom. She used to say she was our mother and father because she had been a nurturer and a protector for us while growing up. But even on a day as fragile as this, she would not give herself permission to break.

In low tone, we begin to recite the 23rd Psalm: *The Lord is my shepherd, I shall not want. He makes me lie down in green pastures; He leads me beside the quiet waters ... Even though I walk through the valley of death, I fear no evil for you are with me ...*

They fire two more shots. Fear withholds us from opening the door. Finally, we huddle close-knit while Mama reaches for the door. She opens it slowly as we begin to exit our home.

I hold tight to Mama. This is all surreal. I cannot believe it is happening. Months prior, there were casual reports on the news that rebel leader Charles Taylor and his "freedom fighters" had taken over Nimba, a rural county in north central Liberia. They were burning villages, torturing and killing people. Reporters said they were advancing toward the city, but some of us didn't really believe them. It was all too hard to swallow.

Life had been good in the capital streets of Monrovia. Nightclubs and other businesses had not stopped booming, although prices for essentials like rice, oil and gas were inflating by day. Other than that, things seemed normal. I guess the ruling government at the time, Late President Samuel Doe's administration, was doing a plausible job at concealing details on Taylor's agenda — the sort of things governments do when they say they don't want to alarm citizens.

So people were going about their lives as usual, and unless you had political edge, no one saw this coming. I suspect that even those who were aware, to some extent overlooked the chances of it happening so soon.

The war snuck up on many of us.

Yesterday, more people were drawing buckets of water from the well to store in their houses just in case something did happen. There were long lines at the corner shops and at the local market. The government had issued a curfew and we had to be in our homes by six o'clock in the evening. More rumors began to spread that rebels were coming.

"Put your hands up!" They yell. "Get in a single line."

Our hands are up. My little brother buries his face into Mama's shoulders. He has developed a reputation in our family as a "cry baby." Today, he is hushed. Silent. It must be God because we do not get any pouting from him.

We walk in single file as ordered; Mama is our leader. My great uncle follows closely behind her. The rest of us deliberately lag until they scream at us again. Then we speed up. It is a tropical day outside. A slight breeze is blowing Mama's tulips in the yard. They have just started to flower so they are the first thing I notice when we step out from the porch to form a line. The tulips serve as distraction for me to stay calm and keep my mind off the men with guns.

"Tell us your name and tribe," one rebel commanded.

He is wearing a vicious frown on his face, almost as if it's a mask to shield him from his boyish facial features. If it is, it does not work. Now standing about two feet away from him, all of us can tell that he is only a young man empowered by that gun. Young men, young women and children were starting to join the rebels and fight in order to survive.

We're in a perfect line facing them when they tell us to identify ourselves individually. They start with my great uncle. His answers do not violate any of their hidden codes so they move on to Mama. I have made my way next to her. Curiously, I begin to sneak glances at the rebels until I fear that I might catch their eyes; then I quickly shift my head downward.

"Thelma Davies," she asserts. "I am Congo."

I lift up my head to look at Mama. Her native affiliation is correct, but her maiden name is not Davies. I am not sure why she's being dishonest with them, but I gather that it may be for our own protection. My mother's family name is associated with prestige and status in Liberian culture. Some of her relatives were executed in a coup ten years earlier because they held positions under a former regime in Liberia. One of her brothers had even escaped and lived in exile in London. As a result, Mama did not want to admit to any association with her last name. She was afraid that rebels might falsely link her to her family's history, even though she had never held any position in past government there.

Ever since I can remember, Mama had been an entrepreneur. She was a hard-working woman who had done honest work running her own restaurant to support her family. But they wouldn't have been able to separate her profession from her family's political history if she had been honest with them. We would later find that it's what many people had to do in the war so that they could survive — deny their identity and rehearse a new one.

Still standing there next to Mama, I am preparing answers in my head for my turn in case they ask me. But once she has spoken, they pass me. I do not know why. "Maybe it's because they think I'm too young," I reasoned in my head. Later, after it is all over, Mama tells me we are blessed that they skipped me because I would've told them my full name.

"And Sweetie," Mama says to me softly, her hands holding up my flushed chin. "If they knew your last name and my last name, we would've all been killed." Then she explains that Kamara is a common name among the Mandingo tribe. The Mandingo people are of Muslim heritage. Apparently, they are killing Muslims, too.

"So from now on, we will go by the last name, Davies," she coaches me. She tells me that Davies is a neutral name, not associated with power or with the tribal conflict. "If anyone asks you what your name is, what will you tell them?"

"Erica Davies," I declare. No particular expression is on my face. I am still trying to make sense of the complication of chaos surrounding me so I have no extra words. But later that night, my belly is full of thanks when I think on her comment. God is certainly with us.

In line, the rebels continue probing my family with questions about their background and beliefs. They ask my sisters if they have boyfriends.

"They are my little girls. No boyfriends," Mama sternly interrupts. I can tell she is taming her tongue from making some smart remark. She is over-protective of her girls. The men refrain from going further with personal questions. They demand we take off our jewelries and hand them over.

"Who owns the house?" they ask. Mama raises her hand. They tell her to go hurriedly inside and bring them "every cent" she has. She runs to her bedroom and brings them a portion of the money she has been saving, hiding the remainder under her bathroom rug.

"You sure this is all you got?" The rebels are adamant.

"Yes, that's all," Mama says. "Please let us go."

"I could kill you and your family right now, but I won't do it," one of the men says in prideful tone. "I asked your neighbors about you and they said you were nice people."

"Besides, I know you," the other fellow points his finger at Mama.

They introduce themselves as Otis and Mulbah. Otis tells her that once before, he was hungry and she gave him food to eat. He tells her he remembers when people do good things for him. Mama does not remember the Good Samaritan act, but we are all thankful it has spared us today. Her kindness will spare us many more times during the four years spent in the war, before we immigrate to the United States.

"You better get out of here as soon as day breaks," they warn us. "Things will only get worse."

They dismiss us. The dark sky hovers over us. As they leave, we fumble inside our home. To avoid being hit by a stray bullet, we crawl on the cemented pavement leading to Mama's bedroom. We assemble and squeeze under her bed. We lay there singing spiritual hymns in whisper. It is a way to tune out the deafening sound of weapons and noise of soldiers combating in the streets. Those hymns would imbue us with hope in the hopeless years to follow.

I lay down wondering if my other sister is okay. Silently, I pray. I want it to be over. I want to return to the life I had yesterday.

Tonight, we have escaped death and the fact that we are still here and breathing, is enough for me.

Revolutionaries Don't Fall From the Sky
Crystal Irby

The voice of Ossie Davis
Over
Film faded pictures
Background credits roll
And I wonder
What mother is this
What faith and prayers made love
To create a sphinx
A needed knight
Whose honor and morality I pray for in my mate
What widowed woman is this
That racism conquered her sanity
Made mother's bond a broken/distant memory
But held long enough
Laid enough foundation
For a future revolutionary's playground
So I pray
To someday
Hold a little lioness in my hands
With the arms of a man
Who feels 10ft tall
Although I wasn't fairytale little girl
Who had wedding planned by 12

Penmanship Books

I knew my womanhood/my marriage/my motherhood
Would be the womb of revolutionaries
Set my eyes on freedom early on
Shook shackles off
Mind/heart/spirit
Didn't buy
Families/2.5 children/no grandmother near
Should be white picket fenced in
Because revolutionaries aren't quite sure
What fences are for
Whether they keep children safe
Or grow up guarded
Afraid to engage the world
As they must to change it
And we
With frustrated breath
Await
The changemakers
As if they will descend from heaven
With an ultra white light
Beaming upon an anointed head
Though they are a gift from God
I know
Revolutionaries don't fall from the sky
They'll come from me
Just as they came from Louise Little/Septima Clark/Dorothy Brown

Pushing them into the world

Praying that violence and fear are absent

On the day their courage is tested

That the price of fight/freedom

Won't be martyrism

That death will come late...wait

For them to see the fruit of their fight

Praying that these daughters and sons

Will find the ink

To unmute the voice

Of women/mothers

Who gave/give birth

To freedom/equality

Yet remain

Nameless/faceless/wordless

Always

Hidden in corners/behind men/between lines

Bearing children

As proof of their existence

today i am breathing

Crystal Irby

today
i am breathing
just to see if i can, without u
i will not call
i will not see you
i will push thoughts of you into tomorrow
it has nothing to do with you,
      my breathing
      has everything to do with me
i will not shut myself out of my life to make room for man
i will stay... this time
because last week, i left
my friends couldn't find me in front of their faces
they did not know
this frazzled woman transforming into love sick girl
holding her breath, turning blue
waiting on your phone call

i'm scared
i may lose you
but i must risk it
to preserve myself
if you don't hear from me

don't take it personal
please know
i believe we will fall in love, last forever, lay and share shame
but
i can no longer live only
in your presence
the thought of you can't be
the only filling that eases hunger pains
i must eat
real food/prayer/self love
i forgot   i have answers
     i forgot   i am worthy
it has nothing to do with you
it's all the basics
typical: daddy abandonment issues
having two beautiful sisters
living in hollywood
never being asked to the prom

but i promised
i would not function out of fear and desperation again
i would not validate myself based on man's ability to give
i would not judge you based on the ghosts of lover's past
i would not hold you accountable for their mistakes
i would not stand beside you
swallow my words/hold my emotions hostage

handcuff myself to fight the temptation to touch you
i promised/prayed
hail heart full of grace let God be
with me the next time i fall in love

I understand we don't get over everything
we learn to allow God to deal with us
show us how to
handle/please understand
i am ready for love

learning that our clocks are not always synchronized
this is our beginning
our own love poem
it may be different from all others
i just need a moment

before i come out of hiding
own everything i am
claim everything i want
take a deep breathe
before i fall in love
this time

Le Serpent
Akua Doku

Le Serpent
Sous l'herbe, dans vos bois
Serpent, que vous êtes espiègle je crois
Est-ce que vous êtes devenu si sauvage
Que vous faites du mal aux innocents?
Serpent, pourquoi est-ce que vous ne pouvez pas être sage?

Under the grass, in your forest
Serpent, I believe you are mischievous.
Have you become so savage that
You bring harm to those who are innocents?
Serpent why can't you be well-behaved?

sad girls
Megan A. Volpert

i wanna take three pills and go to bed early
because that is what sad girls do
i wanna crawl under a rock in my two room apartment
drink cheap white wine from the box
permanently residing on the bottom shelf of my lukewarm fridge
because that is what sad girls do
i wanna wear black all the time and hide my face behind my hair
look at my feet and keep my hands on my hoodie pocket
because that is what sad girls do
i wanna sit by myself german philosophy book on hand
and smoke broken cigarettes in the drizzle
because that is what sad girls do
i wanna say i stayed in because i was feeling sick
but i was really crying all night alone in my room
or crying half the night not alone in my bed
because that is what sad girls do
i wanna eat the same thing for lunch every day
break some plates just to make noise
treat my houseplant like it's a child
and forget what my natural hair color looks likes
because that is what sad girls do

i wanna try to be positive and goal oriented and fail

His Rib: Stories, Poems & Essays by Her

i wanna try every new antidepressant on the market
and never find a good enough therapist
i wanna keep a hundred journals that no one will ever read
wake up sweaty and screaming when i dream about my past
wake up sweaty and screaming when i dream about my future
and faithfully change my joke of the day desk calendar each morning
because those are the motions that sad girls go through
i wanna look in my high school yearbook and find nothing
i wanna look in my wallet and find nothing
i wanna look in the mirror and find nothing
i wanna scratch my wrists until they turn red
to get used to the idea of a bathtub filled with blood
but i can't
because i am a POET
and sad girls go quietly

Penmanship Books

Harlem

Radhiyah Ayobami

Summer in Harlem and he awoke to the shouts of children and the beat of rubber balls against the brick wall of the building. There was no aloe incense burning by the altar near his bed, and no Coltrane or Ellington weaving musical loops through the house. The sun was high above the bamboo window shades, and Folami's dress was folded at the foot of bed. Her sandals were near the door. It took him a minute to pull himself up from bed. Najii didn't like furniture, and their mattress rested on a straw mat on the floor. At first, he hadn't liked it. But at night, when the moon drenched their room in white light, and the shadows of leaves spread and clung along the walls, and Najii's breasts were like maple syrup, he came to love it all.

He walked into the kids bedroom. Folami was asleep on the mattress she shared with Teferi. The cloth had been tucked around her neck and her rag doll with the cornbraids was beside her. Beads of sweat pooled in the peach rows of Folami's scalp. He picked her up and carried her down the hall and into the kitchen. By the time he reached the window, she was awake. Mama, she said, rubbing her eyes. Where's Mama? he thought, as he twisted one of her braids around his finger. Mama, she said again, and pointed to the refrigerator.

He looked at it. Teferi's school schedule and drumming schedule covered half of the fridge, a flyer from a poetry café they had visited was next to that, and a menu from Vegetarian Times, Najii's favorite restauraunt, was stuck near the bottom. He kissed the top of Folami's damp head and walked towards the window. Where was Mama?

He pushed the window up and stuck his head out. Harlem was built on hills, and he could see all the way down the block, past the knot of boys on the concrete steps, and the girls jumping double-dutch with telephone wires, their braids and beads flying and the pop of the ropes on the sidewalk dancing in his ears, past the A train station on the corner where the man stood with his bundle of incense and his tiny glass bottles of homemade oil, and the bodega where the teenagers stood with hands in their pockets, caps pulled over their eyes. The wide streets were already clogged with buses, cars and yellow cabs, but he didn't see her in a cab or on the street or anywhere.

Folami scrambled out of his arms.

Mama, Mama, she said, pointing to the refrigerator. Her bangles jingled as she pointed her round arm towards the fridge. Maybe she was hungry. He walked towards the fridge and started to open it. Half-buried underneath Folami's swim schedule was a note written in crayon.

Kanye-

Had to go. Tried to tell you. I love you love you love you.

Take care of the baby. Back soon. – Najii.

Had to go. Tried to tell you. He ran to the bedroom and looked in the hemp basket by the door. Her dresses were gone. He opened the closet, and saw her sweaters and jeans still folded on the top shelf beside his. He went back into the kids room and searched the wicker basket in the corner. Folami's dresses were folded at the bottom. Teferi's African outfits were missing, but his winter coat and boots were in the closet as well. Had to go. He heard Folami crying in the kitchen. When he walked in, she stopped. Tried to tell you. He put some Cheerios in a baggie and got a bottle of soymilk out of the fridge while she sat on the floor in her diaper and watched him. In the bathroom, he tried to brush her teeth but she folded her mouth inward as tears ran down her cheeks. He changed her diaper and put her on a pair of underwear with a happy face on the front. She looked at the smiling yellow face and cried. He put her dress on and tried to button it up the back. She squirmed, cried, and tried to run away from him, so they went out of the door with the dress unbuttoned. Had to go. He carried her in one arm and a bottle of soymilk in the other. Tried to tell you. She held on to the baggie of Cheerios and cried.

He took her downstairs and knocked on Mrs. Ademayo's door. When she opened it, the sound of children laughing and playing was deafening. He saw one of her daughters putting shoes on a little boy, and the other one lining them up into two rows. Thought you weren't coming, Mrs. Ademayo said, as a small boy behind her rubbed his nose into her skirt. Folami reached out, buried her tiny hands in Mrs. Ademayo's afro and cried. Kanye handed her over along with a bottle of soymilk.

Mrs. Ademayo smiled and patted Folami's back. Guess she misses her mother.

He tried not to jump. You seen Najii?

Just this morning. She was off with her bags again. But aren't children funny? It was only last week your wife came to take this child home and she did not want to go.

He touched Folami's back and she balled up her face to cry again.

Had to go.

I'll be back to get her later, he said.

Don't worry about us women, you know we are unpredictable. She will be fine. Mrs. Ademayo's laughter trailed him down the hall.

Tried to tell you.

Back in the house, he pulled the shades and rolled a joint. He sat on the floor across from their bed and dropped his ashes into a ceramic ashtray Najii had made in her latest art class. He was glad she wasn't around to see him smoking in the morning. He wanted to look for the pipe, but she kept it somewhere in that room where she had her books and her papers and her computer, and he didn't want to touch her stuff even though she was gone. Back Soon. Had to go. She kept the pipe in her writing room because she said joints made her too high, and she didn't want to sit at the computer and zone out. With the pipe, she could take a couple of hits during the day and still think. In bed, they liked to smoke joints. They would pass it back and forth, lying naked on the print cloth and listening to Bob Marley. By the time Bob got to Redemption song, the joint had burned down to a roach and their eyelids were heavy. She didn't like to smoke down to the end because she said it made her throat sore, so he finished it and left the last bit in the ashtray. Then with warm hands and cold bodies, they wrapped in the print cloth and went to sleep, in the shelter of that single bed.

    Tried to tell you.

A year ago, when he and Folami were living with his mother, and Najii and Teferi were living with her mother, he went to her building on a Sunday afternoon and called her from the window. Her mother didn't allow company on Sundays. She came down, fresh from church, in a spring-yellow dress and white headwrap. He wanted to kiss her. He took her hand and led her around to the parking lot at the back of the building. Folami was growing, walking and talking, and soon it would be time for her to go to school, he said. Teferi would be in kindergarten, and it was time for him to find a good school too, he said. His divorce was final and his wife hadn't even asked about Folami, he said. She calls you Mama, and anyway, it's about time, he said. She put her hands on the back of his neck and looked up into his face. Okay, she said.

That Friday, she had a day off from school and he took a sick day from work. They met downtown and went to a Justice of the Peace on Court Street. Later on, they took the kids to a Jamaican shop across the street from his mother's house and toasted Ting bottles to celebrate. The kids cheered without knowing why. At the end of the month, when they were still living apart and Najii's smiles and homemade dinners had become less frequent, he came to her house one afternoon when her mother was away and said it was time for them to move. She kissed the top of his head and ran to get the map she kept in her top drawer. The walls of her room were covered with pictures; the Golden Gate Bridge in San Francisco, the water blue and cloudy underneath, a couple of palm trees against a pink sky in Miami, a beach covered in miles of white sand in Gulfport, Mississippi, two children about Teferi's age playing barefoot on a hill of red dirt in Alabama, a little girl standing naked in the doorway of a house in Antigua, and a group of smiling village people with matching beaded necklaces in South Africa. He sat on her bed with the map in his hand and she curled beside him, waving her hand at pictures that he hadn't even seen before. Where do you want to go? she asked, and her eyes were like diamonds. He hadn't seen that

Penmanship Books

smile since the day in the parking lot. Where do you want to go?

The map was still unfolded in his lap. He put one hand over it. Well, Brooklyn, he said. I want to go to Brooklyn. She pulled away from him, and her face closed. Brooklyn? You're in Brooklyn already. He tried to reach for her hand, but she moved further away. I like Brooklyn, he said. Your mother's here, my mother's here. There's always somebody here to watch the kids. You got school. I got work. In a couple years, I can get a transfer. Wherever you go, people need mail. Anywhere, where would we go? She looked at a picture he had never seen before, it was of a naked pregnant woman with locs down her back, standing alone in a grassy field, with the branch of a huge, gnarled oak tree hanging over her. She looked at the picture for a long time. Yeah, she said finally. Where would we go.

They went to Harlem. He searched for ads in the newspaper. He made all the phone calls. He went to see the apartments alone. When he found an apartment, he signed the lease first and told her second. She didn't seem to mind. She was always busy, on the Internet looking at schools she wanted to go to, or places she wanted to visit, or she was in her room with her notebook, and when she had her notebook, she wasn't talking. He bought a car and drove his and Folami's clothes to the new apartment, and she kept laying on her bed, writing in her notebook, collecting her places to live. When it was in the middle of summer, and he had already paid two months rent on the apartment and still hadn't moved in, he came to her house one day with a couple of boxes and four extra-large garbage bags. Pack, he said. She packed and sighed, sighed and packed. When he came back the next morning, she was asleep on a pile of old blankets and her and Teferi's clothes were still in the drawers. He packed for her, and drove them all up to the new place on a Sunday. School was out, and she didn't have anywhere to go. She stayed in the house all day with Teferi and Folami, cooking and cleaning and sewing outfits for the children on the old sewing machine his mother had given her. In the evenings, when he came home, they took long walks on the slopes of Harlem, watched the domino games on milk crates and cardboard tables, and bought gelatos from the Mexican woman with her white cart. The children liked to stand right beside her and watch as she shaved the ice off in vigorous back and forth motions, and dumped the shredded mess into a plastic cup. Teferi's favorite part was choosing a flavor, and he lingered over the glass bottles like a man selecting fine wine, first hovering over the neon-yellow lemon, then motioning towards the light-green lime, and finally choosing the bright-red cherry, which was the only flavor he would eat anyway. When everyone had their cups of liquid slush, they walked up to the Catholic church with the huge stone steps and ate in the shadow of the Virgin Mary, and they were all at rest.

Those were the good evenings. On the bad evenings, she moped and fried sweet potatoes for dinner and nothing else, and she refused to go out, and instead sat barefoot in the kitchen complaining about how she missed her mother and her friends and that if he had to move her away from home, at least he could move her someplace different and exciting, and not just the same old city, with the same old things, an hour away. On the Saturdays when he had to do his route and came home too tired to go walking with his family, she put the kids to bed early and had her nights out. She had a friend in the Bronx, only a half-hour away on the train. The friend was a stripper and occasional hooker with five sons, and whenever she came to the house she was always dragging one kid by the collar and smacking him, and smoking on a cigarette. Her kids pulled stuff out the cabinets, ran over the woven mats in their sneakers, and left broken incense sticks on the floor. Whenever Najii went to the Bronx for her Saturday nights, she came back smoked out; her eyes red and strained, her clothes wrinkled, her voice hoarse and scratchy. Once, when she was out too late to come home and arrived back early Sunday morning, she came into their room and undressed and he saw she had glitter on her titties. He jumped out of bed and grabbed her, pushing her against the wall. Where you been? he asked. He squeezed her arms until it seemed like he could feel her heart beating through his hands. Where you been? What you done? He slammed her into the wall and she was crying and saying she hadn't done anything. Teferi was banging on the door and yelling and Folami was crying in the hall. He grabbed the cloth from their bed and rubbed it hard over her breasts, scraping the sparkles off and leaving red streaks across her skin. Hear the children, he said, as he slammed out of the room and left her crumpled against the wall, crying and covering her breasts with her arms. From then on, they went for their walks every

Penmanship Books

weekend, and there were no more Saturday nights.

By the time the leaves on the tree outside their window begin to curl, he had switched his route from Brooklyn to the Upper West Side, and he was less than an hour from home. Teferi had been enrolled in Harlem Prep, and Najii could walk from home to his school in fifteen minutes. Folami was going to Mrs. Ademayo three days a week. Najii was the only one who would ride the train to Brooklyn twice a week for school. He didn't think it was a good idea, with him down on the West Side and her in Brooklyn, there was no one to get to the children in a hurry. What if Folami was in one of her moods and couldn't stop crying? What if Teferi had an asthma attack and needed to be picked up from school? She shouldn't be all the way in Brooklyn. So she walked Teferi to school and took Folami downstairs to Mrs. Ademayo and dragged them back and forth to drumming lessons and swim class and ignored the letters and postcards-register now!- from her school and spent her days shopping for fresh food and making sure Kanye had clean and ironed uniforms hanging in the closet every morning. Some nights, after dinner, when the children were asleep and he laid on the low mattress watching the shadow leaves shake and waiting for her to come, and then she came, her shirt sleeves pushed above her elbow and the wet spot on her belly from washing dishes, and she looked over at him before reaching for the joint that rested between his fingers, he saw a blankness in her eyes that hadn't been there before. He hadn't called her eyes diamonds since they had left Brooklyn. Don't you like it here? he asked, as they lay side by side, their upper arms and thighs touching. I'm all alone here, she said. I could understand leaving to do something, but to go and do nothing. You take care of the kids, the house, that's something, he said. He passed the joint to her and she inhaled, holding her breath for a long minute. Besides, he said, how can you be alone when you got me?

The longer they lived in Harlem, the quieter she became. She went for long walks alone when he came home, and he worried about her walking the hills in the winter blackness, her headphones plugged into her ears, her hat pulled down. Would she even see anybody coming? When she wasn't busy in the house, she closed herself in the computer room and did her writing. Their first Christmas in Harlem came with a swiftness like all holidays in New York, and before they knew it, the stores were crammed with dolls and toy trucks, and Teferi was begging for a Christmas tree, his mother and hers were calling asking when they could come and see the new place, friends they hadn't talked to in months were inviting themselves over and sending out invitations in return, and there was food to be cooked, outfits to be made, and the house had to look presentable. Najii was forced to order a small divan for the living room against her will, so their mothers would have somewhere to sit, even though she gave it away after the holidays, and their friends came and sat in their socks on the Persian rugs, admired the bamboo window shades and ate couscous out of wooden bowls with their hands. When their children and all the visiting children had flopped down to sleep in another room, someone would break out the chronic and Kanye would bring out his old drums, and everyone smoked and danced and laughed until dawn. During the holidays, she stopped her evening walks. She left the door open to the computer room when she went to write. She slept on Kanye's chest when she went to bed, and he no longer had to go to sleep staring at her back. But when all the festivities were over, and the house was quiet and bare again, the divan gone along with the guests who had sat on it, and Harlem was just plain old Harlem again, with the knot of teenagers in front of the store she hated to pass and the urine smell of the A train in the mornings, and her days stretched out, a long litany of cleaning cooking washing sex children cleaning cooking washing- then, she started going for her walks again, and the door to the computer room was always shut.

As the after Christmas bills started clogging the mailbox, Kanye began leaving the want ads on the kitchen table every morning for her. He talked about the merits of work and how much sooner they might be able to move to one of the places that she had kept on her bedroom wall and now kept folded in a shoebox under the bed. Every night he hauled out his drums and played something for his family, and Folami stumbled around in her diaper, slapping her fat feet on the floor. See, I have talent too, he said. But that don't mean these kids don't have to eat. Bills have to be paid. Writing is good, real good. But you have to take care of home first. She said, I don't go to school. I don't visit my friends. I stay in the house and take care of you, and that's all right. But if I don't write, I'll die. And I'm not willing to die for you. He didn't leave any want ads for her the rest of that week. The next week, Teferi had a school trip, and Kanye said he couldn't go because they didn't have enough money. Najii gave him some of the money she kept tied up in a headcloth at the top of the closet, and she slammed into the computer room and didn't come out for the rest of the night. He slept alone in the big bed and felt as if he had been abandoned in the house. In the morning she was gone, and he had to drop the children off. That evening, she came back in a white collared shirt and a pair of black pants. He hadn't seen her in anything but print dresses for so long that he almost didn't recognize her. She walked stiff in her new clothes, like they were strangling her. I got a job at Staples, she said. Making copies and stuff. I'll be home for the kids. She never said anything else about the job, like about some coworker that never stopped talking, or some manager that timed her break, or maybe a customer who was rude because she mixed up his copies. He spied on her once, on his lunch hour. He borrowed a jacket and hat from his friend and rode the train uptown in the middle of the day. He squeezed through the crowded store with his head down, pretending to look for something. He stood behind a mother with a couple of kids who were knocking some folders off the shelves and watched her. She had on a blue and white plastic nametag, and she was putting papers in an envelope. She didn't look sad or happy or anything. He thought about walking up to her counter and surprising her, but he didn't know if that would make her smile either.

Soon, the leaves were green and flat again, and she had been at Staples six months. The computer room was filled with Folami's baby swing and stroller. Kanye kept his drums in one corner, and Najii's stories were under a heap of outgrown clothes and toys. She went out with a few friends from work sometimes, and came home smiling and a little tipsy, and they spent weekends together or with one of the grandmothers. She hadn't talked about school or writing except once, in the spring, right before Folami's second birthday. Teferi was cutting pictures out of a magazine, and he looked at a picture of a beach in Hawaii for a long time. They hadn't been to the beach since moving to Harlem. It was just too far. Najii saw Teferi looking at the picture and said, it won't be long now. Kanye looked at her. He wasn't planning on taking a vacation anytime soon. She looked him straight in the eyes and said, I told you I wasn't dying for no one. That was in April. In May, she was gone.

Now that he had taken Folami to his mother's, the house was empty. He roamed the halls like a troubled spirit, trailing a line of smoke behind him, and thought of her when they were seventeen and he had seen her in the park on the swings with her friend, she had on a headband and some socks and he probably went to the Catholic school across the street and wasn't into giving up the cat or getting high, but he loved the way her peach lips turned up when she laughed and how her thighs smooched together on that swing seat and he talked to her anyway; and that summer he had taken her in the apartment he had back on Flatbush Avenue, high above the street, on the sixteenth floor, and they spent afternoons in his twin bed, watching the sky and listening to the traffic down below, and when the sky was purple it was time for her to go, and he was surprised by how sweet and easy her loving was, there had been no virgin drama, and then came college and they drifted, he married a girl in his biology class and she had a baby with a guy he saw on the corner, and when her baby was walking good, he ran into her in the street and said, hey, and they told themselves it was just hey, but hey, a few years later he was divorced with his own child, and it was only natural that they got together, after all, they had been together all along anyway.

In that dark house, her presence came to sit with him and stayed. He saw their radiant walls at night and the pattern of leaves across her belly, her blackberry nipples in his mouth, he heard Coltrane and saw the curls of coconut incense hanging in air, he heard the sigh of her pleasure in his ear, and it lingered there, and when he went to work and the other guys asked him to hang out, he heard her sound and shook his head and said nah, I got to go home, and the older men smiled and said, there's a man that loves his woman, and they didn't know his woman was gone, and at night when he turned alone in the big bed, he felt her straddling his back, rubbing lavender oil between her palms and saying, be still, as she kneaded his back like the biscuits she made on Sunday mornings, and he saw her at the stove in her wrap cloth and flip-flops boiling rice, and in the kitchen on the low stool with Folami braiding her hair, and the wet cloth smell of the old iron on his uniforms, the clack of the hangers when he slid them aside each morning and picked the best pressed one to wear, and evenings in the chair by the window, her standing in back of him, his head against her warm belly as she greased his scalp, the sound of the comb through his hair like static, and after she had patted it into a nice little afro, she always dipped her fingers in the grease and massaged his hairline, and bent and kissed him on the forehead when she was done, just as if he was one of the children, and to think she had done this while she didn't like him, and maybe even hated him, and that all the time she had been unhappy and miserable when he had been so happy, and when he thought of these things he wanted to lay down and not get up, and that's what he did.

When the laying-down period was done, he got up, packed a bag and showered. He went to get Folami from his mother's and she clung to him and cried, and then he went to his cousin in Brooklyn and borrowed a car. He drove back to Harlem and waited. He went back to work and dropped Folami as Mrs. Ademayo. He cleaned the house and gave her baths and tried twice to cook a pot of rice and ended up burning it, and then he went down to Vegetarian Times and ordered some dinner. Folami cried when she smelled the familiar food and Najii was nowhere around, but he rocked her on his knee and fed her tiny bites until she was calm. They lingered in the restaurant until it closed, listening to people talking and eating and not wanting to go back to the empty house. On the twenty-third day after she had gone, she called. He was sitting on the bed with Folami in his arms, next to a flickering white candle. Where are you? he asked. Miami, she said. By daybreak, he was on the road to Florida.

concrete thought
Felice Belle

like most
i want the real thing
and am afraid of getting it

like a monet
you are best viewed from a distance

i pull away for an aerial view
you (eyes closed
lips pursed) are beautiful

and i did not say i could spend every saturday
afternoon stuck to you only

skin and sweat separating our bodies
bathed in july breezes blowing in from

the backyard sometimes makes
me forget this is brooklyn

at your side limbs entwined
counted the gray hairs on your head

Penmanship Books

you left behind half-eaten strawberries
and promise of next time
i'm certain my sub-conscious
premeditated the biting of your bottom lip

in the mirror you examine it
i say, it's not as if you play a horn
my mo' better blues reference is missed
like you will be

minutes later
you leave

me alone

your scent
on my sheets

the remainder of the day
i will be concrete
sidewalk after a sun shower

saturated
      slowly

evaporating

un pequeño sueño (for gabriel)
Felice Belle

sunday washing dishes
in brooklyn kitchen
heard rufus wainwright sing *barcelona*

      one year later i arrived
thought i had seen the sun rise
from back seat of yellow cab
drunk rides from lower east side
to crown heights
new years day saw sun
rise over mediterranean sea
for first time
saw sun rise
met him at dawn

formerly of fort greene
by way of east la
now resides in spain
archangel gabriel
with virgin mary tattoo
named bar after graffiti crew
and cali area code, *dostrece*
two a.m.

kitchen was closed
he found bowl
fed cold steak and fries
to three stateside sisters
weary from walking la rambla
being mistaken for prostitutes
dodging champagne bottles thrown at dome

he hates new york
eats only raw food
i love brooklyn
and hamburgers
buy carrots now
he ocean away
made homesick me want to stay
brush up on my castilian spanish
learn catalan
made me want to lay in bed
for a week
get high
listen to prince b-sides

instead have photos
empty space
cold air
oleta adams singing *get here*

Infidelity
Suzi Q. Smith

it feels dirty,
cheating on myself with you
    (take another drink and laugh)
put my spirit on silent
know it will be angrily awaiting my return, so I avoid going home
 practice
fast-talking   accusations and lies,
hope accountability gets lost in the fight,
slam the door behind me covered ears, closed eyes
I'm not accustomed to this
business of deception and fear
cold-sweat-shaking at the heaviness here,

sometimes I want to sear your hand into my flesh
maybe then I'll feel less
alone (facing myself)
I'm drowning   in a sea of band-aids
wading my way towards matter, I
can't remember what matters
 Jimi Hendrix says: *"the only reason people care when you die*
is because they haven't stopped using you, yet"
so I'm sorting through bounced checks,
trying to collect empty promises

wrap myself in receipts,
shout "This is what you told me!",
embalmed in what you owe me,
and I – mummy,
not sure if I still breathe
but walking just the same,
running hard and fast from the consequence of faith . . .

I stare emptily into the mirror, ignoring the affair
tiptoe 'round my expectant gaze,
pretend I'm not there
my conscience traces empty words, her finger in the air
but I know where
 the landmines are tucked beneath my tongue

it feels dirty
cheating on myself in search of matter,
I   am
disintegrating   is-   land
no matter,
throw another box of band-aids in the ocean to buy some time
 don't weep for me
I belong to the sea
and soon will fade your image of me,
already this moment's a memory
as I return to me

His Rib: Stories, Poems & Essays by Her

Marguerite Porete to Hillary Rodham Clinton
Marty McConnell

"Nature demands nothing which is prohibited."
from *The mirror of simple annihilated souls and those who only remain in will and desire of love*

oh lady, I know why you stay with him. any woman
who'd be a saint or president's got to have a man
to vouch for her, to swear it's God speaking
and not the devil – and what a woman
he made you. a favor with his pants down,
the best thing that could have happened to you
was his flag-waving infidelity – you went from ice
to *just like us* in the space of a television minute. me,
I'd rather die a heretic than live under the thumb
of some priest, but that's a martyr speaking.
and for that, they stripped the name from my book
for three hundred years. but the words, even the fire
couldn't divorce them from me, from the God-in-me,
*the Soul is satisfied by this nothingness which gives
all things. For the one who gives all, possesses all*

the temptation to power at any price is nothing new –
France in 1306, America 2006, neither
a good time to taunt authority, religious or secular
if there's a difference, neither a good time to stand

Penmanship Books

without your man, or the best of times, depending
on your endgame, what kind of annihilation
you're aiming for, in other times
I would have been beatified, St. Catherine,
St. Juan de le Cruz, we all preached the same doctrine,
the death of reason, absolute submission to our God,
no wrong possible *because all that this Soul wills
is what God wills that she will*

what do you will, Hillary? what lays the tracks
you race, for what will you enter
the fire? some things don't change, Hillary,
so long as you've got ovaries and a throat
and choose to use the latter you're a threat
without need of any other weapon
– but you know that, don't you, the stake's
just the thing for us, you know there's a bullet
with your name on it or worse, a lover
in Boston, that woman you swear to silence
every visit

your secrets are safe with me, Hillary. Marguerite
of Hainault called La Porete, your sister in tongue,
strongly suspected of heretical depravity, fuck
their oaths. when they haul you before some false
and festering court, remember me. disdaining
to seek absolution, obstinate in these rebellions,

oh they called my book, that divine ink, a pestiferous
lie, I don't know of what they will accuse you, perhaps
that man will buy you enough time to shift the tide,
to make the bench your own, to alchemize
pain into power or gold, but one hundred years
to the day from my fire came Joan's, Hillary,
to endure the fire you must become
the fire, become the fire before they turn it
against you, there may be time left for you,
for all of us anonymized and shunned
into dust, the second coming will be a woman,
they burned that book on first reading, be
the third, Hillary, make your body the pyre
in which they, this time, burn.

miniature bridges, your mouth
Marty McConnell

what we do in the dark has no hands. no
crossover effect, no good-bye kiss
after the alarm. what we carry in,
we carry out, end of story. this
doesn't even want to be love. except
in minutes when your face
has the shape of my palm and I think
lungful. let want out with the cat. returns
and returns, something dutiful. persistent.
hold your breath, let it build, let go. this
is practice. I'm losing weight, a bad sign,
I'm happy. *serious*, you say. *contained*,
I think. the cat comes back with a dead bird
to the doorstep, an offering. bloodless
this should be easy. a two-step
to cowboys. you're beautiful
but that's not the point.

2
I know my way back perfectly well. like
the back of my hand, as it were. but look,
the labyrinth walls are high hedge, and green.
this also could be joy.

3

I literally don't know your middle name. does that
matter? what systems we arrange for intimacy, small
disclosures like miniature bridges, your mouth. not
what I'd anticipated. softer. to begin with,
I should tell the truth more. I could miss you,
and that's a liability.

4

I'm not often off-kilter. but you're so
silent, even naked, and almost
absent. I hush too, why
are we here. go. want
to throw things, you,
the clock, break windows
until something bleeds
and you finally scream.
I tell you too much; we are not
those people. or nothing – maybe
I say *utilitarian fuck*. how
would that be. I want you
to want to fall in love with me
and that's unhealthy. wrong.
leave your shoes by the door
and pretend it's the movie. it's love
in the movies it's casablanca and toy story

and water no ice come here. pockets need
to be untucked, drawers thrown open,
nobody's safe. there, I've said it:
somebody I was
could have loved you.

Lizzie Borden's index finger
Marty McConnell

none of the rest wanted to do it. I won.
the axe sang in the basement all night long
-- sharp, enough off-key for us to know
she was waiting, too

some loves come in apron and a thimble's-worth
of remember / some in shirtwaist and whispers
to make you wish you'd never heard your own name

it was the bed that hated that woman, not me.
it was him I wanted, but the sheets hissed
and insisted beneath the flatiron / I did laugh after,

at the thought of it. how they'd find her there
in pieces, how they'd have to burn those sheets.

and him? that was me. the first blow
from behind because I couldn't
have borne it if he looked surprised.

on the second, back wanted to stop.
but arms were all in, blow after blow
the walls so gorgeous the ceiling

grew jealous so drink ceiling red

/ how much have you heard /

when the eye split the handle snapped
and that was it. I checked to see he couldn't
look peaceful. took off that smock
and fed it to the stove

/ she was never your proxy, Mama
and he never her husband and as long
as I sit here quietly folded, engaged
in no mischief

red will do the pointing / for us.

His Rib: Stories, Poems & Essays by Her

Artist Bios

:**ebele ajogbe** : Quirky. Earthy. Nigerian-brown. Heavy-hipped. / Loves mangoes. The feeling of peace wrapped round her dream-tongue. And hugs. / When she's not writing, she's busy saving mango trees from extinction.

:**E. Amato:** is a spoken word artist, writer, and filmmaker. She has been published in THE LION SPEAKS: An Anthology for Hurricane Katrina and Poetic Diversity. She knows Mahogany L. Browne rocks and is amazed and grateful to be included in this group of wondrous women.

:**Cristin O'Keefe Aptowicz**: is a poet and author who lives and writes in New York City. Founder and host of the three-time National Poetry Slam Championship Venue, Urbana. Cristin has authored four books of poetry as well as three screenplays.

:**Radhiyah Ayobami:** is the recipient of a NYFA Fiction Fellowship 2006, a Cave Canem Fellow, and a finalist for the 2004 Hurston-Wright Writers Award. She lives in Brooklyn and is currently working on her first novel.

:**Courtenay Aja Barton:** high school, junior year. sitting in my ap english class, listening to a conversation about the great gatsby. the teacher asked a question, and i knew the answer, but no one else did. i raised my hand and gave the answer. my voice is quiet. apparently, no one else recognized the power of soft voices.

:**Felice Belle:** is a poet, a playwright and teaches poetry and performance workshops for elementary and high school students. She has performed at the Apollo Theater, P.S. 122, the American Museum of Natural History and Rikers Island. She recently

Penmanship Books

completed her first full-length play, Tell the Truth Lying.

:Tara Betts: a writer, performer and educator living in New York. She earned her MFA from New England College, represented Chicago on two National Poetry Slam teams and self-published two chapbooks *Can I Hang?* and *SWITCH*. Tara is a lecturer in creative writing at Rutgers University.

:Tamara Blue: facilitates poetry workshops to youth in Los Angeles and featured on Russell Simmons' Def Poetry & award winning documentary *Sp!t*. She was the 2005 and 2006 Los Angeles Grand slam champion and participated in the Grams Town National Theater Festival in Johannesburg, South Africa.

:Crystal Senter Brown: is a mother, wife, poet, author, singer, songwriter, and Justice of the Peace. Her work has appeared in numerous publications including *VIBE Magazine*. You can find her @ www.crystalsenterbrown.com

:Mahogany L. Browne: is a writer, performance poet, educational consultant, Brooklyn transplant, book publisher, friend, host/curator of the Nuyorican Poets Café, owner of PoetCD.com, co-founder of Jam On It Poetry Show; thinks in run off sentences, likes caffeine, hates to exercise, loves to love to love to love...

:Akua Doku: member of Urbana's 2005 & 2006 National Slam Team, has traveled through Spain, lost her passport, reclaimed herself and welcomed the love of learning French.

:Eboni: My father is a breakbeat...My mother is a melody...I got lost somewhere between the hook and the bridge...You may have seen me on a milk carton...Birthed in the BX...2007 Nuyorican Slam Team Member.

His Rib: Stories, Poems & Essays by Her

:ebonyjance: Activist/Poet/Writer/CHILD OF GOD has a self-published a book of poetry entitled: Young Black Girl and is working on her first fiction novel.

:Falu: is a poet, teacher and performer. She was a member of the 2006 Nuyorican Slam Team, ranked 7th in the nation; Highest Ranking Female 2006 and believes in fashion. Seriously.

:Andrea Gibson: is the 2001, 2002 and 2003 Denver Slam Champion. She has been showcased on Free Speech TV, Dyke TV, the documentary Slam Planet, and Independent Radio Stations nationwide. She has released 3 albums and is currently a member of the prestigious Bullhorn Collective.

:Nicole Homer: is the winner of the 2006 Emerging Writers Audience Favorite award at Wordfest 2006, team member of NYC Urbana 2007 Slam team and has opened for the likes of Amiri Baraka and Miguel Algarin.

:Bassey Ikpi: Nigerian mother of a Brooklyn baby boy who inspired poems during a fire scare, mandatory bed rest and his first television appearance on HBO's Def Poetry. He enjoys walking and posing his perfected baby scowl during his mother's daily picture taking frenzy.

:Crystal Irby: as 2004 Los Feliz Grand Slam Champion, 2006 Hollywood Grand Slam Champion (the 2nd female to do it), & member of the 2005 Hollywood Slam Team, (ranked 3rd in the Nation) Crystal focuses on Spoken word to change lives. She has toured South Africa and featured in the documentary Sp!t .

:Amanda Johnston: Cave Canem fellow and Affrilachian poet, currently serves on the board of directors for the National Women's Alliance, is a member of The Austin Project, a co-founder of the Gibbous Moon Collective, and founding editor of *Torch: poetry, prose, and short stories by African American Women.*

Penmanship Books

:April Jones: lives in LA, writes when she isn't working at a television production company. She likes shoes, good poetry, myspace, her friends and herself. She is the coach of LA's Downtown Slam Team.

:Rachel Kann: has toured across America with the Chicks in Arms tour and the SlamAmerica tour, has self published 5 books and 2 CDs and been published in several anthologies. She recently released her first book of short stories, *10*.

:Erica S. Kamara: a journalist and freelance writer/editor living in Atlanta, Georgia. When she's not writing, you can find her indulging in her favorite pastimes: reading, art & photography. You can reach her at kamara.erica@gmail.com.

:Abena Koomson: After graduating from Sarah Lawrence College, I have used writing to exam the constant conflict of my spirit and found many instruments of expression: teaching, trombone, euphonium, trumpet, bass guitar, oil pastels, digital photography, knitting, dance and most of all my voice.

:LV: writes memoir about growing up in Memphis, her grandmothers, motherhood, her husband's death and middle-aged romance. She has been published in Ballard Street Poetry Journal, in Look up in the Sky: Poems about Comic Books and on Rogue Scholars website.

:Marie-Elizabeth Mali: A former acupuncturist and life coach, she writes poems with an eye toward the sacred in the everyday. Her poems have appeared in the online journals, *2River View* and *Hobble Creek Review*. She will begin the MFA in Poetry program at Sarah Lawrence College in the fall of 2007.

His Rib: Stories, Poems & Essays by Her

:Marty McConnell: serves on the Louder Arts Project's executive committee and co-curates the flagship Monday night series. After working with Urban Word NYC, the legendary Norman Lear tapped her to be one of four poets for *Declare Yourself,* a national nonprofit campaign aiming to empower young voters.

:Derrica McCullers: is a fiction writer, hiding in the offices of Sports Illustrated for Kids, during the day. This Baltimore native relocated to Brooklyn and does not like Go-Go music, just in case you were wondering.

:Gabriela Garcia Medina: a Cubana-Xicana who has shared her art, poetry and creativity across hemispheres in Cuba, Brazil, Spain, Geneva, and South Africa. As Artistic Director of the Human Writes Project, Gabriela promotes cross-continental community through performance and culture.

:Caitlin Meissner: as a performance poet she uses her activist background in anti-racism work, disability advocacy and youth empowerment as a platform on the human experience. Caitlin has just released her self-published chapbook, *BRICK/by/BRICK* and EP *Brighter Yellow Than The Morning Sun.*

:Aja-Monet: is one of the youngest Nuyorican Poets Café Grand Slam Champions (2007), founder of Poetry Potluck, an annual fundraiser for Katrina Relief at the prestigious Sarah Lawrence College, Aja has performed with Abiodune Oyewole of The Last Poets, Amiri Baraka and Reverend Run.

:Thea Monyee: has aired on HBO's Def Poetry Jam and BET's "The Way We Do". In 2005 Thea's Black History Month promo was directed by actress, Kim Fields and aired on Nick @ Nite and the TVLand cable channels.

Penmanship Books

:**Jessica Elizabeth Nadler**: an artist whose chosen medium is tongue, pen, page and stage. She a member of the louderARTs collaborative poetry collective 'synonymUS'. She is by way of New Jersey and Brooklyn, now resides and writes on the Upper East Side – NYC. This is her first publication.

:**Lilian A. Oben:** is a West-African born poet and writer of fiction. Lilian has spent her pre-U.S. life living in Ethiopia, England, Kenya, Italy, Morocco, Cameroon and Nigeria. She is a current resident of Washington, D.C., and is working on her collection of short stories which she hopes to publish in 2007.

:**Lynne Procope**: is a poet from Trinidad and Tobago, co-founder of the louderARTS Project and poet in residence with VisionIntoArt, a multi media/multidiscipline performance collaborative which seeks to marry prose, film, poetry, dance and music in collaborations engaging socio-political and artistic discourse.

:**Nicole Sealey:** a writer, editor, and Cave Canem fellow. She has written for a number of arts journals including *Code Z: Black Visual Culture*. Her interviews with acclaimed writers Sapphire and DJ Spooky can be found in *Artists and Influence*: Volume XXV and *Studio*, respectively. She lives in Brooklyn, NY.

:**Queen Sheba:** Rolling Stone's 500 Songs for Kids '07, Featured Poet for the National Edition of Rolling Out Magazine April '07, and Nominated for NAACP Image Award '07. Sheba has been seen on: 106&Park, VH-1, Showtime at the Apollo and documentary Sp!t.. She has been seen with: Kanye West, Floetry, The Roots Crew, Musiq, Amiri Baraka, Saul Williams, and Nikki Giovanni.

:**Nikki Skies:** is a playwright, performer, educator residing in Los Angeles. Her CD *Moody* and short story book, *Mississippi Window Cracks,* have been well received and allow her to facilitate literary workshops for students in elementary school thru college.

:Suzi Q. Smith: I am a poet. I am the author of *Walk Softly (and carry an a.k.)*. www.lulu.com/suziqsmith. Also I am the SlamEmpress for Denver's newest slam venue, SlamNUBA! In addition, I am serving as the Poetry Editor for a beautiful online review, www.denversyntax.com.

:Sydnee Stewart: is a performance poet, actor and writer. She was featured in the documentary Hughes' Dream Harlem, and is a lead actor in the feature film "Everyday People" She performed at the National Black Arts Festival in tribute to Dr. Maya Angelou and Cicely Tyson and is working on a screen play.

:Heather Taylor: a Canadian writer & educator. She has been published and performed throughout Europe, Asia & North America at events & festivals. As a member of the London branch of Malika's Poetry Kitchen, her collection *horizon & back* was published by Tall Lighthouse in October 2005.

:Kimberley D Taylor: daughter of Mary Elizabeth Taylor; granddaughter of Margaret R. Belisle; and great grand daughter of Mary L. Jones.

:Imani Tolliver: is a poet, visual artist, educator, arts advocate and has served as a consultant to community organizations, museums and educators. You can find her work on-line at getunderground.com.

:Kimberly Trusty: a Jamaican Canadian native residing in Birmingham, UK, the poet and playwright has been published in numerous anthologies and released her first collection, *Darker Than Blue* (McGilligan Books, 2002, Toronto).

Penmanship Books

:Genevieve Van Cleve: lives and works in Austin, Texas. She is a professional writer and performer with years of poverty, joy, and "experience" to prove it. Her work concentrates on the finer things, social justice, relationships, feminism, politics, and mendacity.

:Jeanann Verlee: is a poet, prose writer, actor, activist, and recovering punk rocker. She has appeared in numerous anthologies and magazines, holds a BA in Theatre Performance and English, was member of the 2006 New York City Urbana National Poetry Slam Team, and lives in New York City.

:megan a. volpert: is a performance poet with an MFA in Creative Writing from Louisiana State University. She teaches High School English and has featured at over 50 venues the US promoting her CD, *no morning after*. She resides in Georgia and is a board member of Poetry Atlanta.

:jaha zainabu: a writer, painter and mother has published several books including *The Science of Chocolate Milk Making and Corners of My Shaping* (Penmanship Books). She lives amongst the green of Decatur, Georgia.

:Kelly Zen-Yie Tsai: is a Chicago-born, Brooklyn-based, Chinese Taiwanese American spoken word artist who has performed at over 200 venues worldwide including three seasons of "HBO Def Poetry." For more info, www.yellowgurl.com

- ~~Butter~~
- ~~Eggs~~
- Bread
- Waffles
- ~~Cereal~~
- ~~Sausages~~
- ~~Macaroni~~
- ~~Cheese 1.98~~
- ~~Vegetables~~ Birdseye 5 for 5
- ~~Cold cuts~~
- ~~Yogurt~~ ~~Yoplait 10 for 3.99~~
- Juice
- ~~Salad~~
- ~~Pork chops~~
- ~~Wing Dings~~ ~~18 piece Fryer Pack~~
- ~~Chicken Breast~~
- ~~Steak~~
- ~~Ground Beef / Turkey~~
- ~~Strawberries~~
- ~~Pineapples~~ ~~Cameo fruit America 5 for 5~~
- ~~Bacon~~ ~~2.48 Tyson Bacon~~
- Biscuits
- Bread Crumbs
- ~~Hot dogs~~
- ~~Blue Cheese~~ with Bone
- ~~Mayonnaise~~ ~~2.48~~

- ~~Ground Beef~~
- Hamburger Helper
- ~~Waters 5.88~~
- Syrup 2.49
- Toilet Tissue 12/6.99
- ~~Paper Towel~~
- ~~Juices~~
- ~~Cabbage~~
- ~~Carrots~~
- ~~Lemons~~
- ~~Filters~~
- Blueberry Muffin
- ~~Salad Dressing 5 for 5~~
- ~~Vitamin Water 5 for 5~~

~~Get~~
~~Drunk~~